WOW Time

52

ENGAGING CHILDREN'S MOMENTS

MARK BURROWS

WoW Time
Engaging Children's Moments

ISBN 97801426707926
PACP00581001-01

10 11 12 13 14 15 16 17 18 19 - 10 9 8 7 6 5 4 3 2 1

MANUFACTURED IN THE UNITED STATES OF AMERICA

TABLE OF CONTENTS

MUSINGS FROM MARK...

This collection of 52 Children's Moments represents those times when I got the children's attention from the start, kept them engaged throughout, and left them talking about it the rest of the day. *Wow Time* represents what I've learned — from my many mistakes, and from the many beautiful, amazing children I get to see every week.

LESSONS WITH OBJECTS VS. OBJECT LESSONS

I'm always on the lookout for ways to incorporate objects into children's moments. A balloon, a funny hat, or a nativity figure can help make a children's moment more multidimensional. But here's the trick — I have to remember to use the object for what it is, not for what it might represent. If I say, "This balloon is like a person," then I'm doing an "object lesson." Object lessons can get great feedback from the other adults, but I'll lose my younger listeners. Metaphors and similes require a level of abstract thought that most of the children I see simply have not developed yet. That doesn't mean the children aren't very smart. They're brilliant! They just happen to be concrete thinkers at this stage in their development. If I use the words "like" or "as" in my message, I'm going to miss the mark.

CONSIDER THE RANGE

That being said, I will occasionally explore symbolism with children. One reason is that our worship space is full of Christian symbols. Children are very curious about these symbols. "Why is there a lamb on that wall?"

Another reason I touch on symbolism is that we often have a wide age-range of children. It's not unusual for us to have two-year-olds sitting right next to fifth-graders. (We even had a mentally disabled adult join us for several months. We're all children of God.) The wide age-range means that I need to design children's moments to cover that range. This is different than aiming for the average each week. If our average age is six years old, and I gear children's moments to that age, I'm always going to miss the mark with those younger or older than the average.

VARIETY

One week we have a parade around the worship space. One week we go on a treasure hunt. One week we play an interactive game. One week we hear a story. I try never to take the same approach two weeks in a row. A big part of the *Wow Time* experience is the sense of mystery — "I wonder what we're going to do today." All the children know for sure is that they will be safe, they will have fun, and they will learn about God's love.

Compared with some of the examples listed above, simply telling a story may seem stale. But don't underestimate the power of a great story. There are few words that engage children more than, "Once upon a time…"

Take-Homes

Every once in a while I'll have something for the children to take home—a sticker, a balloon, a Chinese yo-yo. But I do this sparingly. One spring, I had handed out take-home objects three weeks in a row. The next week I did not, and some of the children were disappointed. That was my fault. I had set up the expectation that if you come forward for *Wow Time*, you get a prize. There are a lot of important lessons I want our children to learn, but "Church is where I go to get stuff," is not one of them. I usually have a prize for them about every six weeks. That way, it's the exception rather than the rule. The less frequently I give them a prize, the more likely they are to remember when I do.

Two of the take-homes were meaningful because they demanded something of the recipients. One Mother's Day I talked about how important mother figures are in our lives. I showed the children pictures of women in the church, such as the children's minister and the children's choir accompanist. We discussed how each of these women, while not necessarily our own mom, is still an important mother figure because of all they do for us. We then wondered about the women who we might not even know by name, but who act as mother figures in our lives. Each child then got a carnation with the instruction that they must give the carnation to a woman who was a mother figure, but not their own mom. They were also each instructed to find a different mother figure. (Otherwise the children's minister might well have received fifty carnations.) The effect this gesture had on the entire congregation was astounding.

Another meaningful take-home came out of a unique circumstance. One summer I went on a mission trip to Kenya to work with children. Two other members of the mission team and I took over kits for each of the children. The kits had been prepared by the children of our own congregation. Each kit contained socks, pencils, toothpaste, a toothbrush, crayons, and a pad of paper. When we handed out these kits to the children, you would have thought it was Christmas. The children in Kenya wanted to do something to show their appreciation. We suggested that they each use the crayons, paper, and pencils to write short notes with pictures that we could take back to the children in America. The children in Kenya decided to take it a step further. They wanted to become pen-pals with the children in America.

When we returned to America, we made copies of the children's notes as a back-up. Then we gave out the notes during a children's moment, telling our congregation's children how the children in Kenya wanted to be friends. (Here's an interesting aside — I came home with 61 notes from children in Kenya. Guess how many children we had for the children's moment where we passed out the notes? 61! Call it a "God thing!")

We collected the response notes from our congregation's children over several weeks, then sent all of them in one big package over to Kenya. I still have parents come up and remark that this is one of the most meaningful experiences their child has had. Wow!

There is one very practical reason we do take-homes less frequently — it's getting expensive! When we first started adding a children's moment into worship, we would have 10 to 15 children come forward. But we now average over fifty children each week. (We've had over 80 on several occasions.) That's a lot of Chinese yo-yos.

WORSHIP VS. ENTERTAINMENT:

This is a slippery slope. I've seen many a children's moment become little more than an episode of *Kids Say the Darndest Things*. Children might say something that strikes the adults in the room as humorous. The adults laugh, the children see an opportunity for some positive reinforcement, and try even harder to make everyone laugh. And the adult leading the children's moment sometimes acts as a host for the "show," encouraging the children to say and do things for the entertainment of the adults in the room. The children are there to worship, not to serve as comic relief.

Don't get me wrong, I think it's very important for our children to see us smile and laugh in worship, provided that we are laughing with them. But for the few minutes I have each week, my role isn't to entertain the adults. It's to enrich the lives of the children.

A FEW THINGS I DON'T DO:

I don't ask rhetorical questions. If you ask a question, of any kind, to a group of children you are going to get answers, whether you want them or not. In fact, I don't ask too many questions period. I can't tell you how many times a child has surprised me with an answer to a question that I assumed only had one "right" answer.

I don't do a lot of sit-and-listen children's moments. The children have been sitting and listening in the pews already. Why would we call them to the front, just so they can sit and listen some more? Even when I tell a story, the children are actively involved either by making sound effects for the story, or pantomiming the actions.

I don't put individuals "on the spot." Being up in front with all those grown-ups watching can be scary. Even when I invite all the children to sing or say something together, they can be shy. In those instances I ask the entire congregation to join in. It helps the children feel less on display.

I don't shy away from tough topics just because I'm talking with children. If it's All Saint's Sunday, and the senior pastor's sermon deals with death and loss, then I will do likewise, gently and honestly. Our children want more (and need more) than rainbows and butterflies.

I don't start each children's moment with the general niceties like, "How has your week been?" I go right into the children's moment. Of course I want to know how their week went. But that kind of question is best saved for times when I can actually visit with the children.

I don't spend too much time wondering what the adults in the room think. One of the most difficult things about recruiting new people to lead children's moments isn't that they have to talk with a lot of children. It's the fact that they have to talk with a lot of children in front of a lot of adults. One of the things that helps me is to sit or stand facing the children while turned away from the adults. I know a lot of settings where the leader sits at the front, facing the congregation while the children "gather round." I've never found that particularly effective. It creates competition for who get to sit closest to the leader (or farthest away). And it's harder for the leader to see all the children. I know a lot of people like the whole "let the children come to me" look of it all — kind of like the picture of Jesus with all the children. But I'm not Jesus. I'm just the man the children know and trust to teach them about Jesus. When I'm positioned to look each child in the eye, it helps me stay focused on my purpose, instead of on who's watching.

I don't refer to the children's moments I do at our church as "Wow Time" I've been doing these for quite a while. And believe me, I've had more than a few moments that were far from wow-worthy. Let's be honest, they flat-out tanked. Luckily, children are very forgiving, and they come back each week to give me another chance. And they also offer immediate feedback. When I'm delivering a clunker of a children's moment, it's pretty obvious. Ever tried to herd cats?

CELEBRATE

THEME
Palm Sunday is a day when we can celebrate having Jesus in our lives.

SCRIPTURE
Matthew 21:1-11 — Jesus' Triumphal Entry Into Jerusalem

PREPARE
You will need a palm branch for each child. Arrange for someone to help you distribute the palm branches at the appropriate time.

WOW TIME

Let's play a game about some holidays that we celebrate. When I name a holiday that you celebrate, I'd like you to tap your nose. Here we go.

> Halloween. *(Lots of nose tapping)*
> Valentine's Day. *(Lots more tapping)*
> The 4th of July. *(Lots of tapping)*
> Palm Sunday. *(Not very much tapping. There is some tapping, mostly by the children who are enjoying the rhythm of the game.)*

Right, Palm Sunday can be a little tricky. I don't think gift shops sell many "Happy Palm Sunday" cards. But Palm Sunday is a very important day for us. Today we remember a time when Jesus rode into Jerusalem to the waving of palm branches and shouts of "Hosanna!" The people were excited to have Jesus enter their city. And today we can share in their excitement because Jesus is in our hearts forever. And that's worth celebrating!

If you like parades, tap your nose. *(LOTS of tapping.)*

Me, too. Let's have a parade right now. First, you need a palm branch.

Hand out the palm branches. Depending on the size of the group, this may take a minute. In my experience, there are usually a few more children in church on Palm Sunday, so prepare accordingly.

Now I want you to follow me around the sanctuary. I'm going to say a simple chant. Every time you hear me say the word "Hosanna," which means "save now," I want you to wave your palm branches in the air, and say "Hosanna" even louder than I do. Be careful not to wave your palm branch in your neighbor's eye. Congregation, you can help by shouting "Hosanna" with us. Alright kiddos, follow me.

Start walking down one of the aisles of the sanctuary. Let the parade get going for a few moments before starting the chant.

Welcome Jesus into town. Hosanna!
(Children echo as they wave their palm branches.) **Hosanna**!
Take our coats, and lay them down. Hosanna!
(Children echo as they wave their palm branches.) **Hosanna**!
Wave each palm branch. Wave it high. Hosanna!
(Children echo as they wave their palm branches.) **Hosanna**!
Let our praises fill the sky. Hosanna!
(Children echo as they wave their palm branches.) **Hosanna**!

Continue the chant until you and the children have made it all the way around the sanctuary.

CLOSING: *Have the children repeat after you each line of this short prayer.*

Thank you, Jesus
For entering our lives.
Your love
Is worth celebrating.
Amen.

Well That Was Awkward

For years our church struggled with how to include the children in the Palm Sunday service in an authentic way. There had been a long tradition of the children standing on either side of the aisle and holding the palm branches in an arch for the choir and clergy to walk under. Our taller choir members lovingly referred to this as "the gauntlet." Then the children would be quickly whisked to the front of the sanctuary, where their palm branches were frantically taken from them so they could sing their Palm Sunday anthem without distraction. This moment was always very awkward. The children got to hold the palm branches for three minutes, tops. We weren't treating the children like worship participants, but as entertainers with their "prop" palm branches. Something had to change. Saving the distribution of the palm branches for the children's moment where they were used in a more purposeful way made the whole experience more special and memorable for the children. And no one came to take their palm branches away at the end.

THE POWER OF GOD'S LOVE

THEME
God's love has the power to change things for the good.

SCRIPTURE
Isaiah 2:4 — The Future House of God

PREPARE
Acquire one large slinky to use in the lesson, and one small slinky for each child.

WOW TIME

(Play with the large slinky in your hands.) Can anyone tell me what this is? *(Many children will call out, "It's a slinky!")*

I love to play with a slinky. (I can never seem to keep from getting one all tangled up, but it's fun anyway.) Did you know that the slinky didn't start out as a toy? A naval engineer named Richard James was working with springs a lot like this one during World War II. He was trying to make a spring that could be used on a battleship, when one of them fell of his work table. Instead of just rolling on the floor, it did that funny "walking" thing that a slinky does. *(Pause)*

At that moment Mr. James stopped thinking about wars and battleships. Do you know what he thought?

He thought, "I could turn this into a toy. This is something that could make children happy." And that's how the slinky was invented.

Now maybe that spring just accidentally rolled off Mr. James' workbench all those years ago. It's possible. Accidents happen. But what's amazing is that God's love was at work that day. Only the power of love could help a man see a spring, not as equipment for a battleship, but as a toy that could bring joy to millions of children.

Now I have something special for you. I'm going to give each one of you a little slinky. *(Wait for the cheers to subside. It could take a while.)*
And every time you play with it, I want you to remember that God's love has the power to change anything into something good.

Closing

Say the following prayer on behalf of all those gathered.

Thank you God, for starlit nights,
And sunny, joy-filled days.
Thank you God, for loving us,
And teaching us your ways.

Thank you God, for soaring birds
Who daily sing your praise.
Thank you God, for loving us,
And teaching us your ways.

Thank you God, for listening
To every prayer we raise.
Thank you God, for loving us,
And teaching us your ways.

Amen.

It All Comes Back

THEME
If we want to get something (love, respect, etc.) we have to be willing to give it.

SCRIPTURE
Galatians 6:7 — Reaping What We Sow

PREPARE
Acquire enough Chinese yo-yos for each child, and one for yourself. You can get them at most party supply stores.

WOW TIME
Play with a Chinese yo-yo as the children assemble. (Warning: It's REALLY hard to put a Chinese yo-yo down once you start playing with one.)

I love playing with Chinese yo-yos. I think it's so neat how I flick my wrist to send the paper spiraling out. And then – whoosh – it comes right back. We have the power to do that. If we send a feeling or an attitude out, that's usually what we get back. If we send out anger, what do you think we'll get back?

(Most children will answer, "Anger.") If we want to get kindness back, what should we send out into the world? *(Most children will answer, "Kindness.")*

Why don't we try a little experiment to see if that's right? Let's put some kindness out into the world. When I say, "Go," I want you to smile and wave to the congregation. Then let's see what they do. Ready…set…go!

The children smile and wave to the congregation. And thankfully the members of the congregation, with no advance coaching, smile and wave back to the children. As if they could resist.

See. When we put kindness out into the world, that's what we tend to get in return. So if we want a world full of love, laughter, and kindness, it starts with us. To help us remember that we get what we give, I have a Chinese yo-yo for each of you.

(The children cheer.) But I want to wait until after the service to give these to you. *(The children utter a muffled, "Aw...")*

I'm not doing it to frustrate you. It's more as a favor to those sitting in front of you for the rest of the service. Right after the postlude come right up to the choir loft and see me. I have enough for everyone!

The children cheer again. (It's nice to be back on their good side.)

CLoSiNG

Let's close with a call-and-response prayer. I'll say something different each time, but you always respond by saying, "We've got to give it." Let us pray.

If we want kindness,
Children: **We've got to give it.**
If we want patience,
*Children:***We've got to give it.**
If we want respect,
Children: **We've got to give it.**
If we want friendship,
Children: **We've got to give it.**

JUST So YoU KNoW

You are certainly welcome to finish the call-and-response prayer by saying "Amen." Just know that many of the children will follow your "Amen" with their given response, "We've got to give it." That kind of thing doesn't bug me.

THEME
Wonder at God's creation.

SCRIPTURE
Genesis 1:1-31; Psalm 8 — The Creation

PREPARE
Make a poster board sign that says WOW *in big capital letters.*

WOW TIME

(*Keep the WOW sign face down at the beginning.*) We're blessed to live in such a wonderful world. All around us are beautiful sights, amazing animals, and wonderful people. God made it all, and it is good. It's good to be thankful for all that God has given us. And when we see something amazing about God's creation, one of the best ways we can show our gratitude is by saying this word. (*Hold up the WOW sign. Some of the children will say "WOW" without any request from you. And you will have some pre-readers who need a little help.*)

What does this sign say? (*Many children will answer,* WOW. *And now they have helped the pre-readers.*)

That's right, it says, WOW. WOW is an important word. And there sure are a lot of things in God's world worth wowing about. I have an idea. First, everybody stand up." (*Wait for the children to stand. It won't take long. Most of the children I work with are pretty "spring-loaded" as it is.*)

Let's take a trip to the zoo. (*Mimic walking and looking around, and invite the children to do likewise.*)

Now I want you to spot your favorite animal. It might be a giraffe. It might be an elephant. It might be a skunk. (*Some children will call out their favorite. Just roll with it.*) I want you to look at how amazing your favorite animal is, and then I want you to say…(*Hold up the sign.*)

Children say: **WOW!**

Now let's imagine we're each climbing our favorite tree. (*Mimic climbing a tree, and invite the children to do likewise.*) Imagine how it feels to be up in your favorite tree. Maybe there are lots of leaves to hide you. Let's all whisper…(*Hold up the sign.*)

Children whisper (well, most of them whisper): **Wow.**

And we have an amazing church full of amazing people. Let's look out at them and say…(*Hold up the sign.*)

Children say to the congregation: **WOW!**

And you are amazing, too. I know our whole congregation thinks so. In fact, just seeing all of you amazing children up here makes the whole congregation want to say… (*Hold up the sign for the congregation.*)

Congregation, very enthusiastically, says: **WOW!**

WOW is such a powerful word. And guess what WOW upside down is. (*Turn sign upside down. Most of the children will call it out,* MOM!)

That's right. WOW upside down is MOM. Coincidence? I think not. Today, at lunch I want you to look your mom right in the eye, and say, "WOW!" Moms really like that.

CLOSING
Let's close with a call-and-response prayer. I'll say something different each time, and you respond by saying, 'WOW.' Let us pray.

LATER THAT WEEK

For sky and seas,
Children: **WOW!**
For flowers and trees,
Children: **WOW!**

For great and small,
Children: **WOW!**
You made it all,
Children: **WOW!**

Later that week I got a note from a very appreciative grandmother. She had taken her grandson to lunch after church, and at some point he looked at her and said, "Wow." Of all the people in our church, the children may be the best at taking what they learn on Sunday and putting it into practice the rest of the week. Sometimes they just make me want to say, "WOW!"

I WiSH

THEME
Being who we are, and having that be enough.

SCRIPTURE
Genesis 1:26-27 — Made in the Image of God; Psalm 8:3-5; Psalm 139:14)

PREPARE
Review the story.

WOW TIME
This is a short story called I Wish.

Madi was eight-and-a-half. Her little sister Suzann, who hardly ever said a word, followed Madi everywhere.

One day Madi was walking to the park, with her little sister right behind her, when they saw Lola. Lola was wearing a brand new purple tutu.

Madi took one look and said, "I wish I had a tutu like that. Then I could be the best ballerina in the whole world." She twirled around, raised her arms over her head, and skipped down the sidewalk.

Suzann watched her sister, but said nothing.

At the park, Madi and Suzann were playing when a squirrel darted past them, and up a tree. Madi ran to the tree, and jumped as high as she could. But she could only reach the lowest branch. After dangling until her arms gave out, she landed on the ground with a thud. "I wish I could be like a squirrel," Madi said. "Then I could climb to the highest branch of the tallest tree."

Suzann stood there silently.

On their way home from the park, Madi and Suzann walked right by the biggest house on their street. Madi sighed as she said, "I wish I lived in a big, beautiful house like that. It would be my castle, and I would be a princess."

She walked on as Suzann just watched.

After dinner Madi and Suzann brushed their teeth and climbed into their bunk beds. Madi fell asleep as soon as her head hit the pillow. Their mom came to tuck them in. She kissed them both on the forehead, and was about to leave when Suzann spoke her first words of the day. "Mom, I wish I was like Madi. She's an amazing dancer, and she is a great climber, and she's as beautiful as a princess. Madi is awesome."

"She sure is," said their mom. "You both are."

No one could see, but Madi, sound asleep, was smiling and dreaming of being herself, and that it was enough.

CLOSING
Have the children repeat after you each line of this short prayer.

Dear God,
Help me remember
It's not about having it all,
It's about giving my all.
It's not about being the best,
It's about being my best.
Amen.

GOD'S HANDS

THEME
Ours are the hands to go and do God's work.

SCRIPTURE
Ecclesiastes 4:9-10a — Lifting Up One Another

PREPARE
Get an inflatable globe. The size of the globe will depend on your budget and needs. I went online to www.1worldglobes.com and found an inflatable globe that was 39 inches in diameter. It was a splurge, but the wow-factor was totally worth it. Many places offer inflatable globes for under $10. It's totally up to you.

WOW TIME
Place the inflatable globe out of sight at the back of the sanctuary.

Have you ever wondered what God looks like? What do God's eyes look like? Does God have a big nose? And what about God's hands? I wonder what God's hands look like. Well, let's hold that thought for just a second. I want to show you something really cool. I'll be right back.

Trot to the back of the sanctuary humming or whistling "He's Got the Whole World in His Hands." If it's a small inflatable globe, carry it back to where the children are. If it's a really big globe, roll it down the aisle as you keep humming or whistling.

Does anyone know what this is? *(Children will answer, "The world," or "A globe," or "A big beach ball.")*

It's the world. Now, I want to lift the world up. So I'm going to put my hand right here, and lift. *(Place a single hand near the equator and try to lift the world. When it doesn't work, look frustrated or puzzled. And if you are using a smaller globe, adapt this moment to using an index finger rather than a hand.)*

Well that didn't work. I need some help. Would someone like to help me? *(Lots of hands go up, some accompanied by pleas of, "Me, Mister Mark. Pick me!")*

I'm going to pick the quietest hand I can find. *(This almost always works immediately. Plus it reinforces the concept that the loudest doesn't always win. I pick a quiet child, and invite him or her to join me. I have him or her place a hand next to mine on the globe. Then we both try to lift it. It still doesn't work.)*

We need some more help. Let me see who else can help us. *(More hands go up. I select about eight more children. It isn't unusual for us to have 60 or more children at our children's moments. 30-40 is the norm. One of the only drawbacks is that it's very difficult to include every child equally in a moment like this. We can't fit 60 children around the globe, so I have to find other ways to involve the children who don't get selected to place a hand on the globe.)*

I invite all the children selected to stand around the globe and place a hand near the equator (the "middle" for those who aren't sure where the equator is).

I tell the other children that they have a very important job to do. We need them to give us power by clapping as energetically as they can until we can lift the world.

The children start clapping, and then on the count of three, each of the children around the globe presses in slightly, and we lift it up in the air. This not only makes the children clap louder, but the members in the congregation usually clap at this point, too.

Then on the count of three, we put the globe back down and the children who help lift the world go back and sit with the other children.

That was fantastic. Everyone, give yourselves a big round of applause. *(They do.)*

Do you remember before when I asked what God's hands might look like?

At this point I hold up one of my hands and say,

This is my hand, and it can be helpful. But it's not exactly what God's hands look like. All of you raise your hands in the air. *(They do.)*

And everyone here – congregation, choir, clergy – everyone raise your hands in the air. *(Everyone does.)*

See? This is what God's hands look like — everyone's hand working together to lift up our world and make it a better place

CLoSiNG
Sing a verse of *He's Got the Whole World in His Hands.*

RULeS

THeMe
Following God's rules can help us get the most out of life.

SCRiPTURe
Exodus 20:1-17 — The Ten Commandments; Psalm 19:7

WoW TiMe

I sometimes have a hard time with rules. Do any of you ever have a hard time following all the rules? There are so many rules. "Don't run in the halls." "Don't stay up past eight." "Don't put spaghetti up your nose." Rules, rules, rules. Hey, I have an idea, let's play a game. *(The children cheer. They always do when I say, "Let's play a game.")*

Okay, ready? Go!

The children stand there staring with a "now what?" expression. Some children might jump around, but the overwhelming majority has no idea what to do without any additional guidance.

Hm. That's not a very fun game is it? I'll tell you what, I'll add one simple rule – do exactly what I say.

Stand up. *(The children stand up.)* Sit down. *(The children sit down.)* Stand back up. *(The children stand up.)* Raise your arms. *(The children raise their arms.)* Put your arms down. *(The children lower their arms.)* Look up. *(The children look up.)* Look down. *(The children look down.)*

You get the picture. It's important to do this for a good amount of time so the children will get tired of it.

Well that's not much of a game, is it? You're just doing whatever I tell you to do. And while that's fun for me, I bet it's pretty boring for you. *(Some agreement from the children.)*

I have an idea. Let's add one more rule. This time, do whatever I say only if I start with "Simon Says." If you don't hear me start an instruction with "Simon Says," then don't do whatever I'm asking you to do. Got it? *(The children offer a very excited "Yes!")*

Here we go. Simon Says stand up. *(The children stand up.)* Simon Says tap your nose. *(The children tap their noses.)* Stop tapping. *(Some children stop tapping. There are many giggles and even a "You got me, Mister Mark." Then we resume the game. And no, we do not eliminate players in children's moments. There is no "out.")*

Continue playing. Don't be afraid to be tricky. The older children will appreciate this, and the younger children will have a blast either way, especially since there's no "out."

Isn't that interesting? When we started, there were no rules at all, and the game wasn't much fun. Then we added one rule, and it was a little better, but not by much. Then we added yet another rule, and we had a great time. See? The rules are what made it fun! God gives us rules like the Ten Commandments, not to take all the fun out of life, but to help us get the most out of life. Those rules make our lives even better!"

CLOSING
Have the children repeat after you each line of this short prayer.

God is caring, God is kind.
Giving love and peace of mind.
We can follow God's own way
By sharing, caring every day.
Amen.

Note
Our senior minister was embarking on a sermon series based on The Ten Commandments. And some of those commandments are more than a little tricky to discuss with children. Believe it or not, I did a corresponding children's moment for each Commandment. Let's just say that some went better than others.

WRitten on OUR HeaRts

THeMe
When God puts something in our hearts, it's there forever.

SCRiPTURe
Jeremiah 31:31-34 — A New Covenant

PRePaRe
Acquire an Etch-a-Sketch®. Use the knobs to draw some kind of picture on it before the children's moment. I drew a picture of the front of our church building. Okay, it didn't look much like our church, but there was a door and a steeple. It did, however, take up most of the etch-a-sketch screen, so the children knew that at the very least, I'd spent a lot of time on my picture. This will have an impact during Wow Time.

WoW TiMe
I love making pictures with my Etch-a-Sketch. *(Hold up the Etch-a-Sketch so they can see the picture.)* Does anybody know what this picture is? *(The hope is that the children will know. In my case, nobody knew what it was until I told them. One child did think it was a castle, and that wasn't entirely discouraging.)*

I spent a lot of time working on this picture. It's really hard to draw anything curvy with an Etch-a-Sketch. What do you think would happen if I shook it? *(Most of the children know the answer. "It will make the picture disappear.")* Let's just see if you're right.

I shake the Etch-a-Sketch. This is accompanied by some gasps from the children. When I show them the screen, the picture is gone – nothing but a blank screen.

It's gone. When you use an Etch-a-Sketch to make a picture, or write something, you can always erase it. But some things don't go away, not matter how hard you shake. Let's all stand up and put our hands over our hearts. *(The children stand with me, hands over their hearts.)*

God has put a message in each of our hearts. It's a message of love, and nothing we do can ever make the message of God's love for us go away. Let's try to erase the message. Everybody rub where your heart is.

(*Children rub their hands on their chests over their hearts. You will need to model this, especially for the younger children.*) Now let's check and see. (*Put a hand to your own heart and invite the children to do likewise.*) No. The message of God's love is still there.

You are welcome to ask the children to answer if the message of God's love is still there. Most children will answer, "Yes." But some will say, "No." Remember, if you ask a question you never know what answer you'll get back.

What if we try to shake that message out? Everybody shake. (*The children all shake their bodies.*) Now let's see if the message of God's love for us is still there. (*Put a hand to your heart again, and invite the children to do likewise.*) Yes. God's love is still there! What if we try to hop it out? Everybody hop. (*The children all hop.*) Let's check it one more time. (*Everyone puts hands to hearts.*)

You know what? That message of God's love for us is still there. When God puts something in our hearts, it's there forever. We can try to erase it. We can try to shake it out. We can try to hop it out. But God's love will always be in our hearts.

CLOSING
Invite the children to repeat after you each line of this prayer.

We may not always see you, God,
But we still know you're there.
We feel you in the warming sun
And in the cooling air.

We feel you all around us, God,
Beneath, beside, above,
For you have filled us with your message,
Filled us with your love.
Amen.

FOLLOW THE LEADER

THEME
We should follow Jesus' teachings and example.

SCRIPTURE
Luke 18:22 — Come, Follow Me

WOW TIME
Let's play "Follow the Leader." I'll start. Everybody follow me.

Start marching slowly down one of the aisles. Let the children catch up to you. Do all sorts of other things such as hopping, waving arms in the air, skipping, or walking in super slow motion. Make sure the children are following you.

Next you can choose one of the children to lead. This is a risky move, but if you know your children, you should be able to avoid major insanity. (We all have that one child who would have us all climbing the pulpit. There are many times where that child will make an excellent helper. This is not one of those times.) Depending on time, you may decide to choose a few different children to lead.

Then be the leader again yourself, and the lead the children back to the front (or wherever the children's moment takes place for you).

That was fun. I love playing "Follow the Leader." Sometimes it's fun to lead, and sometimes it's fun to follow. During Jesus' life he asked his friends to follow the leader. And guess who the leader was.

Most of the children say, "Jesus." (This is a pretty low-risk answer. Sadly, it seems that we've conditioned children that the answer to any question we ask them in church is either "Jesus," "God," or "love.")

Just imagine what it would be like to play "Follow the Leader" with Jesus as the leader. We could always trust that Jesus was leading us the right way. Jesus was very kind to others. Can we follow Jesus' lead and be kind to others? *(The children say, "Yes.")* Jesus helped the poor and needy. Can we follow Jesus' lead and help the poor and needy? *(The children say, "Yes.")* Jesus made sure no one was ever left out. Can we follow Jesus' lead and make sure we never leave anyone out? *(The children say, "Yes.")* Jesus really is a leader we can follow.

CLOSING

Let's close with a call-and-response prayer. I will say something different every time, and you respond by saying, "We will follow Jesus." Ready? Let us pray

Will you follow Jesus?
Children: **We will follow Jesus.**
Even when times are tough?
*Children:***We will follow Jesus.**
Even when things get rough?
Children: **We will follow Jesus.**
When you're sad and fearful?
Children: **We will follow Jesus.**
When you're hearts are cheerful?
Children: **We will follow Jesus.**
Will you follow Jesus?
Children: **We will follow Jesus.**

HELPING HANDS

THEME
Hands are for helping, not harming.

SCRIPTURE
Luke 10:25-37 — The Parable of the Good Samaritan

WOW TIME

God gave us our hands for very special reasons. Can you think of any? *(Invite the children to volunteer reasons they think God gave us our hands. One child might say, "For waving.")*

Waving — that's a good one. Why don't we all practice. Let's wave to the congregation. *(Have the children wave to the congregation.)*

Can anyone think of something else we can do with our hands? *(One child might say, "High fives.")* Sure, high fives are great. Everybody high five your neighbor. *(The children will get into it. Make sure the children do it gently. Some will try to high five their neighbor's hand off.)*

What else can we do with our hands?" *(Allow a few more children to offer ideas, such as "hugs," "holding hands," or even "making silly faces." Invite the children to act out each one of these.)*

Now, nobody said, "God gave us hands for hitting." God certainly doesn't want us to use our hands for that. You gave such great answers. I can think of one more. God also gave us our hands for praying. Let's fold our hands and pray together. Repeat after me.

CLOSING
Have the children repeat after you each line of the following prayer.

Thank you God,
For giving us hands,
For holding,
For healing,
And for helping.
Amen.

Note

Sometimes I'll open up a portion of the children's moment to questions, fully aware that I have little control of the answers. But when the majority of the children's moment is based on responses from the children, it gets a little risky. I was very lucky that no child said, "Hands are great for picking your nose," or some similar response. Just remember that when you ask the children to volunteer responses, what you get back might surprise you.

Even When Nobody's Watching

THEME
Doing what Jesus wants us to do, even when no one else is watching.

SCRIPTURE
Matthew 7:12 — The Golden Rule

PREPARE
Provide a TV remote, a small sheet of bubble wrap, a small individually wrapped snack for each child (it could be a granola bar or small box of raisins).

TRUE CONFESSION
Okay, when I did this one I used donut holes. I know, I know, it's just deep-fried dough with sugar. But they are small, and there's a donut shop perfectly centered between the church and my house. Most times I try to have a children's moment written by Monday or Tuesday. That way I can play with ideas, hone things a bit, and gather any materials well in advance. But I have to confess I was having a bad case of writer's block with this one. It didn't all come together in my head until about 11:00 P.M.... Saturday Night! If I had thought of it even a few hours earlier, I would have had a healthier option than donut holes. Oh well.

WOW TIME
Today we're going to play a game. I'm going to act out a scene, and I want you to tell me what you think Jesus would want me to do. Got it? *(The children enthusiastically respond, "Yes!")* Here we go.

One school morning I get up, and I'm the only one awake. Mom and Dad are still asleep. I walk into the living room and see the TV remote. *(Pick up the remote and hold it.)* Mom and Dad have told me that they don't want me to watch TV on mornings when there's school. They say I should read a book instead. But they're both still asleep. If I just watch TV for a little bit, no one will ever know. What would Jesus want me to do? *(Most of the children will quickly reply that I should not watch TV. When I did this children's moment, one child nailed it. "You should put down the remote and pick up a book!" Way to go, kiddo!)* That's right. I should probably do the right thing and put down the remote, even though nobody's watching.

Okay, here's another scene. One afternoon, after school, a package comes to the house. Inside the package is... bubble wrap. *(Pick up the sheet of bubble wrap and start popping the bubbles.)*

Ah, I love that sound. Popping bubble wrap is one of my favorite little pleasures. And my brother likes doing it as much as I do. But he's still at soccer practice, and won't be home for an hour. You know, I could pop all the bubble wrap and throw it away before he gets home. No one would ever know. What would Jesus want me to do? *(Most children will say something like, "Save some of the bubble wrap for your brother.")* You're probably right. Okay, I'll save some for my brother. *(Put the bubble wrap down, if you can).*

I've got one more scene. Let's imagine I just got to the church and I find five dozen donut holes. Nobody's watching. I could eat all five dozen donut holes myself, and no one would ever know. What would Jesus want me to do? *(Children will respond with something like, "Share the donut holes with your friends.")* Are you sure? *(The children are sure, "Yes!")* But I really like donut holes. *(Children may insist, "You should share them!")* Well, as usual, you're right. Jesus would want me to share all those donut holes with my friends. Well, guess what, friends. It just so happens that I really do have five dozen donut holes. *(The children smile, cheer, and clap. They know what's coming.)*

And since Jesus would want me to share these donut holes with my friends, that's exactly what I'm going to do. I have enough for everyone. And I also have just enough sense to not pass out individual donut holes right this second. *(This next part is specific to our setting, but it at least offers an example of what you could do. Feel free to adapt this to whatever works best for your setting.)* I've given four bags to Miss Lindy to take to the Sunday school rooms. Those of you going from here straight to Sunday school can get your donut hole from her. And I will keep one bag here in the sanctuary. If you go from here back to sit with your family for the rest of the service, I'll have a donut hole for you. Make sure you come see me right after the postlude.

CLOSING
Invite the children to repeat after you each line of this short prayer.
Dear Jesus,
Help us to do,
What you want us to do...
Even when nobody's watching.
Amen.

A Look in the Mirror

THEME
Remember who you are, who made you, and who you are supposed to be.

SCRIPTURE
2 Samuel 12:1-15 — Nathan Condemns David

Yep, that's right! The senior minister chose to do a sermon on David, Bathsheba, and Nathan's condemnation of David's actions. This is quite possibly the most child-UN-friendly story in the entire Bible. It's in the Top Ten, anyway. But not being one to back down from a challenge, I took it on.

PREPARE
Provide a small hand mirror and several hats that you can wear, one on top of the other. The hats I used were a baseball cap, a plastic Viking helmet, a cowboy hat, a stocking cap, and a birthday hat. The key hat here is the plastic Viking helmet. When you're wearing one of those, you can put on at least three more hats — one on top of the helmet, and one on each horn. Use whatever hats you have, the wilder the better.

WOW TIME
Once there was a boy named Dave. *(Put on baseball cap.)* Everyday he would take a look in the mirror, *(Look in mirror.)* and say this prayer:

Let there be peace on earth,
And let it begin with me.
Let there be love on earth,
And let it begin with me.
Let there be kindness on earth,
And let it begin with me.

Since Dave wanted to live in a world that was peaceful, loving, and kind, he knew he had to be peaceful, loving, and kind.

One day Dave stood up to a bully who was not peaceful, loving, or kind. This made Dave very popular. Over time, Dave became so popular that he kind of let it go to his head. He stopped taking a look in the mirror each day, and even became a bully himself.

One day on the playground, Dave saw a kid wearing a hat. Even though Dave already had a hat of his own, he wanted that kid's hat. So he just took it. And he put it on. *(Put on another hat, on top of the baseball cap.)* Now Dave had two hats, but do you think he was satisfied? *(The children answer, "No.")* Dave wasn't satisfied at all. He saw another kid wearing another hat. He wanted it, and he took it. *(Put another hat on top of the others.)* Then he took another hat, and another. He didn't care whose feelings he hurt. He just wanted those hats. *(Put more hats on, as many as you can without them falling off.)*

Then one day Dave saw a boy named Nate wearing a really cool hat. He wanted that hat so much and told Nate to give it to him. Nate just looked up at Dave and giggled. "What are you laughing at?!" Dave roared. "Don't you know who I am?" Nate answered back, trying not to laugh, "I know who you are. Um, Dave… when was the last time you took a look in the mirror?" Dave responded, "I don't need to look in the mirror. I'm Dave! I know how awesome I am!" Nate chuckled, "Seriously, dude. Here's a mirror. Take a look." *(Hold the mirror up and look in. Act shocked at what you see.)*

Dave was shocked. "What have I become?" he cried. "This isn't who I'm supposed to be." He felt awful. One by one, he took off the hats and gave them back to their original owners. Each time he offered a very heartfelt apology. Dave even found a girl who didn't have a hat and gave her his own baseball cap. Then he apologized to God for not being the best he could be. After that, he never forgot to take a look in the mirror each day and say this prayer.

CLOSING

Turn so you are facing the same direction as the children. Hold up the mirror so that all of you are looking at it. Invite the children to repeat after you each line of Dave's prayer.

Let there be peace on earth,
And let it begin with me.
Let there be love on earth,
And let it begin with me.
Let there kindness on earth,
And let it begin with me.
Amen.

WHEN BAD THINGS HAPPEN

THEME
Sometimes bad things happen to good people, and there's no one to blame.

SCRIPTURE
Matthew 5:45b — The Rain Falls on the Just and the Unjust

PREPARE
Legos® or other plastic blocks, enough for each child to have at least three individual blocks. I use the extra large size to avoid any choking hazard issues. I made individual 4-piece sets of blocks with one piece of each color (red, blue, green, yellow), and the same kinds of pieces. It was worth the extra work.

WOW TIME

One time my Nana came to visit. I know Nana always loves me, even when she can't visit. But her visits are special. On this visit Nana gave me my first-ever set of blocks. I played with them the whole time Nana was there, and way after Nana had to go back to her home.

One Friday night I made an airplane out of blocks. I was very proud of it, and couldn't wait to show it to my friend Sid the next day. So I put it on the coffee table, and went to bed.

The next morning I went into the living room to look at my plane. But it was all in pieces on the floor. My little brother, who was two years old, had taken it apart. I was really upset and I wanted to blame someone.

I wanted to blame my little brother. But it wasn't really his fault. He was just acting like a curious two-year-old. I wanted to blame my Nana. She's the one who gave me the blocks. But it wasn't my Nana's fault. She only wanted me to be happy. I even wanted to blame myself. But it wasn't really my fault either. How was I to know my little brother would take my plane apart? There wasn't any warning on the box about little brothers taking planes apart.

About that time I heard the doorbell ring. It was Sid. He took one look at the huge mess on the floor and asked, "What happened?" I told him about the plane that I'd made, and that I couldn't wait for him to see it. But unfortunately, my little brother took it apart. "Let's build it again," Sid said. I asked, "But what if I can't remember how?" Sid answered, "Let's build it again, anyway." "But what if my little brother wrecks it again?!" I protested. Sid said, "Let's build it again anyway." So we did.

Sometimes a plane falls apart, and it's nobody's fault. We can spend all our time trying to find someone to blame. Or we can spend that time building, and before we know it, we'll have a new plane.

(Bring out the individual block sets.) I have a new little set of blocks for each one of you. *(Big cheer from the children.)* Now here's your homework assignment. Every time you play with these blocks I want you to remember that when something falls apart, you have the power to build it again. It may never look the same as it used to. Build it anyway.

Closing
We're going to close with a call-and-response prayer. I'll say something different each time, and you always respond by saying, "We'll build it anyway." Let us pray.

When something we care about falls apart,
Children: **We'll build it anyway.**
Even if we're not sure how,
Children: **We'll build it anyway.**
Even if it takes a really long time,
Children: **We'll build it anyway.**
Even if the work is hard,
Children: **We'll build it anyway.**
When it would be easier to blame someone,
Children: **We'll build it anyway.**

Note
We had a guest preacher for this service. I asked him what his sermon would be about so I could match the theme during the children's moment. He told me I shouldn't bother since his sermon would be asking the question, "Why do so many horrible things happen to good people? Why do so many innocent children suffer?" This was an incredibly challenging topic. If I ever shy away from an issue in a children's moment, it is because of my inability to distill its essence in a way that is meaningful for children. But I never underestimate their abilities or their faith when it comes to dealing with these issues. So I gave it a shot.

BEST BOOK EVER

THEME
The Bible is full of amazing stories that teach us about God's love while capturing the imagination.

SCRIPTURE
Joshua 1:8 — This Book (also Romans 15:4)

PREPARE
Bring a Bible.

WOW TIME

How many of you like stories about ships out on the sea? *(Some children will raise their hands or say, "Me, me.")* Let's all pretend we are out on a ship. Let's raise the sail. *(Pantomime raising the sail, and have the children do likewise.)* Now the waves are getting really rough, and the ship is rocking back and forth. *(Sway back and forth with the children.)*

Do any of you like stories about animals? *(More children respond.)* Let's all pretend to be some different animals. Everyone roar like a lion. *(Roar with the children.)* Now let's baa like sheep. *(Baa with the children.)* Let's buzz like bees. *(Buzz with the children.)*

Does anybody like stories of showdowns out in the desert? *(More children respond.)* Let's have a hopping showdown. I'll count "One, two, three." On "three" we'll see who hops first, me or you. If you hop first, you win. Ready? Here we go. One… two…… THREE! *(Let them hop just ahead of you.)* Okay, you win.

Now guess what. There is one big book that has all of these kinds of stories and hundreds and hundreds more. Can you guess what that book is? *(Many children will shout out, "The Bible!")*

The Bible, that's right. It's got stories about shipwrecks, animals, showdowns, mysteries, treasure hunts, and parties. The Bible has something for everyone. It's the best book ever!

CLOSING

Let's close with a call-and-response prayer. I'll say something different each time, and you always respond by saying, "Best book ever." Let us pray."

A story about a rainbow,
Children: **Best book ever.**
A story about a baby in a manger,
Children: **Best book ever.**
A story about God's love for us,
Children: **Best book ever.**
A story about how we should treat each other,
Children: **Best book ever.**

FaitHFUL FRieNDS STiCK TOGeTHeR

THeMe
Through good times and tough times, true friends are faithful to one another.

SCRipTURe
Ruth 1:16 — Where You Go, I Will Go

PRePaRe
Provide a small brass bell for each child with the clapper pulled out. You can find small brass bells at many craft stores, or by going to www.brassbell.com. Use needle-nose pliers to carefully pull the clapper out of each bell. The clapper is usually a piece of circular metal attached by a wire. Pull the wire out as well so that there is nothing to make the bell ring.

WOW TiMe
Before beginning the story, teach the children the phrase "faithful friends stick together." Have them say the phrase with you each time it occurs in the story.

Once there was a group of faithful friends who went out on a journey. As they walked down a path, if one stopped to tie a shoe, they all stopped because **faithful friends stick together**.

They walked along until they came to a village market. They all stopped together to have a look around because **faithful friends stick together**.

They saw a man with a collection of little brass bells. He gave each one of the faithful friends a bell. They each said "thank you" and the man skipped merrily on his way." *(Hand a small brass bell to each child.)*

The friends thought it was such a generous gift… until they tried to ring the bells. When they did… no sound came out. They shook the bells. *(Invite the children to shake the bells.)* No sound. They blew on the bells. *(Invite them to blow on the bells.)* No sound. They even tried tapping them with their fingers. They could hear a little sound, but it wasn't at all what they hoped the bells would sound like. *(Invite the children to tap the bells with their fingers.)* So the friends sat down, trying to figure out what to do.

A boy came up to one of the friends and said, "Psst. Do you want to come with me and play in a new band? You can bring your bell. It doesn't have to ring. It looks so cool." The friend thought about it, then said, "No thank you. I'll stay here with my friends, because **faithful friends stick together.**"

A girl came up to one of the other friends and said, "Hey, we're about to play kickball, and we need one more player. Do you want to join us?" The friend said, "No thank you. We got these new bells and we're trying to figure something out." The girl replied, "But those bells don't even ring. Who wants a busted bell anyway?" "I don't know," responded the friend, "but I do know that **faithful friends stick together.**" So the girl ran off to play kickball, leaving all the friends there to figure out what to do with their bells, because **faithful friends stick together.**

"Together… That's it! Together is the key!" one of them finally said. "What if we hold our bells just so…" (*Show the children how to hold the bells by the handles with the bell itself facing upward, almost like a hand bell.*) … and tap them together?" And so, very gently, the friends all tapped their bells together. (*Invite the children to tap bells with each other. Have them try many different friends around them, not just one other person. The sound should be somewhat like wind chimes. As you finish telling the story, have the children play the bells very softly underneath. There's no sense trying to get them to stop tapping the bells.*)

It was the most beautiful sound the friends had ever heard. If they had all gone in different directions, they never would have heard it. But that day, they made beautiful music, all because **faithful friends stick together.**

Closing

For our closing today, I would like you to play the bells very softly, and listen as I pray aloud for us. Let us pray.

When faithful friends stick together,
This world becomes a better place.
When faithful friends stick together,
Church bells ring.
When faithful friends stick together,
Beautiful music is made,
God's music.
How wonderful God's world can be,
When faithful friends stick together,
Amen.

Yikes! Time

This children's moment was originally based on our senior minister's sermon series on The Ten Commandments. And this was the one for "Thou Shalt Not Commit Adultery" Sunday. As you can see from the Scripture reference above, I've offered a less thorny alternative.

THREE THINGS

THEME
There are three things we can say that are great ways to honor our parents.

SCRIPTURE
Exodus 20:12 — Honor Your Father and Mother

BALANCING ACT
I know a lot of people, parents mostly, who can quote this Bible verse from memory. Interestingly, many forget the words from Colossians 3:21: "Fathers, do not provoke your children, or they may lose heart." Just like all relationships, it's about balance.

PREPARE
Using index cards, make a card for each child with these three sentences:

1. How was your day?
2. I love you.
3. I know you do.

WOW TIME
Honoring our parents is important. It's something God wants us to do. And there are many ways we can honor our parents. Today I'm going to teach you three simple things to say that will truly honor your parents.

(Hand a card to each child.) On each card is written three sentences. Would anyone like to read the first one aloud? *(Many children volunteer, including a few who can't read yet. I choose one with a "quiet hand." She reads, "How was your day?")* Let's all practice that one together. *(Lead the children in asking, "How was your day?")*

I know when I was a kid, my parents would ask me this every single day. And I always had plenty to say about my day. But you know what? I don't ever remember asking my parents how their day had gone. When we ask our parents about their day, we're showing that we care about them and their feelings. They certainly care about us and our feelings. Asking parents about their day is one way we can honor them.

Would someone like to read the next sentence? *(Many children raise their hands. I choose one. He reads, "I love you.")*

Notice that it doesn't say "I love you, too." I always said, "I love you, too," to my parents, because they always said "I love you" first. The next time you see one of your parents, be the first to say, "I love you." It is a great way to honor your parents.

Who would like to read the third one? *(Many children raise their hands. I choose one, and the others are disappointed because they know it's the last one. Assure them that every week there will be a new children's moment and new opportunities. And then back that up by always trying to choose different children. That can be difficult to do, because there's always that one kid who will give the golden answer to any question you ask. And then there's that one kid [I was this kid] who will take the children's moment all the way down the rabbit hole.)* The third child reads, "I know you do."

When our parents tell us they love us, they are doing it for the most wonderful reason in the whole world — they want us to know that WE ARE LOVED. If we say "I love you, too," right back to them, sure they like that. But that's not why they tell us they love us. They want us to know that we are loved. And so, when a parent says, "I love you," one of the best things we can say back is "I know you do." To raise a child who knows he or she is loved is one of the greatest honors a parent can ever have.

Let's practice that one. Everyone in the congregation is going to look right at you and say, "I love you." Then I want you to respond with the sentence we just learned. *(Have the congregation say, "I love you," to the children. They will do this most enthusiastically. The children respond with, "I know you do.")*

Keep your card with you. Practice these three sentences every day until you have them memorized. That's one great way we can honor our parents.

CLOSING
Invite the children to repeat after you each line of the following prayer.

We love you God,
And we know you love us, too.
We love our parents,
And we know they love us, too.
Amen.

Healing Words

THEME
When we hurt someone's feelings, there is something we can do to help them feel better.

SCRIPTURE
Proverbs 12:18 and James 5:16 — The Healing Power of Words

PREPARE
Provide a new Band-Aid® (latex-free) for each child. Children love bandages, especially since pictures of cartoon characters began appearing on them. Many children (including my own two) seem to wear them as accessories.

WOW TIME
(Hold up a Band-Aid®.) Does anybody know what this is? *(Most of the children will respond, "A Band-Aid®.")* That's right, it's a Band-Aid®. Most of us have had to wear one of these before.

How many of you have ever had to wear a Band-Aid® because you skinned your knee? *(Most children will raise their hands. Don't be surprised when a few show you the Band-Aids® on their knees or elbows.)* How many have ever had to put a Band-Aid® over a cut finger? *(Most children will raise their hands.)*

Now here's a tricky one. Have you ever had a time when your feelings were hurt? *(Most children will again raise their hands.)* Did you try to put a Band-Aid® on your hurt feelings? *(A child might say "yes" to this. And really, who's to say that isn't true? Most children, however, will probably say, "no." Validate the children, acknowledge the comments, and move on.)*

When my feelings have been hurt, I didn't think a Band-Aid® would work. And when I've hurt someone else's feelings, I don't think a Band-Aid® would make them feel better either. But the good news is, when we hurt someone else's feelings, there is something we can do that might make them feel better. We can try to make them feel better by saying these two simple words — I'm sorry. Let's practice that. *(Lead the children in saying "I'm sorry.")*

Those are two very important words we can say when we know we've hurt someone's feelings. It might make them feel better right away, but sometimes it takes a while. Even if it doesn't make them feel better right away, it's still a good thing to say.

(*Give each child an individually wrapped adhesive Band-Aid®.*) I want each of you to take one of these Band-Aids®. You never know when one might come in handy. And when you look at these Band-Aids® I want you to remember the power of saying "I'm sorry." You never know when that might come in handy.

CLOSING
Invite the children to repeat after you each line of this short prayer.

Dear God,
Help us realize
When the best thing to do
Is to say, "I'm sorry."
Amen.

WOW Time OVERLOAD
Saying "I'm sorry," truly is an important, even empowering thing to be able to do. On the other hand, I've seen children, and adults, apologize when they really did nothing wrong. They were simply more worried about keeping the friendship, or the peace, than they were about personal pride. This is a complex issue, and I wanted nothing more than to delve into it. But oh my! How much can you pack into one children's moment? Sometimes I have to remind myself that there are 51 other Sundays in a year, and that I simply can't cover all aspects of an issue in one five-minute segment.

Don't Forget the Invitations

THEME
Jesus calls us to be an inviting people.

SCRIPTURE
Matthew 4:18-22 — Fish for People

PREPARE
Provide a blank invitation and envelope for each child. Place the invitations perpendicularly in the envelopes prior to handing them out. First, this will save time when you're handing these out. Secondly, if you stuff the invitations all the way into the envelopes, some of the children will be tempted to lick and seal their envelopes. Trust me.

WOW TIME
Let's imagine we're getting ready for a big party. First, let's blow up some balloons. *(Lead the children in pretending to blow up some balloons.)* Next, let's hang some streamers. *(Lead the children in reaching up and pretending to hang streamers.)* We need a cake, right? Let's decorate the cake with icing.

("Pink icing!" one child says.) Okay, pink icing is fine. *(Another child calls out, "And sprinkles!")* Sure we can put sprinkles on the cake. *(More children want to offer suggestions. I need to get control of this.)*

Many of you have great ideas for what we can put on a cake. On your way home from church today, I want you to imagine your perfect cake and what you would put on it. If you like, you can make a picture of it and bring it to show me next week. Okay? For this cake right now, let's add pink icing and sprinkles, and they can be whatever color sprinkles you want. *(Lead the children in pretending to add pink icing and whatever-color-we-want sprinkles to our cakes.)*

Now we're ready for the party. *(Take a big pause and follow it with a gasp.)* Oh no! We forgot the invitations! We did all this work. We blew up balloons. We put up streamers. We decorated the cake. But because we didn't give out invitations, no one will come to our party.

What if that happened here at church? The children's choir works hard to make beautiful music. The Sunday school teachers do their best to make the lessons fun. But we can't forget to invite people. When we have something really special, like our church, we need to share it. And we can't share our church with others if we forget to invite them.

This week, I want us to practice being inviting people. I'm going to give each of you a blank invitation and a blank envelope. You can use your invitation to invite someone to our church. Or you can invite someone over for a play-date. Or you can invite your mom or dad into the living room for a picnic on the floor — just as long as you use that invitation to invite someone to do something with you.

CLOSING

Have the children repeat after you each line of the following short prayer.

Thank you, God,
For making us feel invited.
Now it's our turn,
To make others feel invited, too.
Amen.

IT'S NOT ABOUT FiSH

The "fishing for people" story is so evocative. I kept trying to find ways to work fish or fishing into this children's moment. But I realized it's not about fish. It's about inviting others into relationship with God. Jesus used the fishing analogy because he was talking to fisherman. I wasn't talking to fishermen. But I was talking with people who have been to a lot of birthday parties.

TWO POWERFUL WORDS

THEME
Knowing when to say "Thank you" is very important.

SCRIPTURE
Psalm 92:1 — It Is Good to Give Thanks

WOW TIME

Today we are going to explore two very powerful words. And when you know how to use these powerful words, you'll be stronger than Superman… *(Have the children flex their muscles.)* And more wonderful than Wonder Woman…*(Lead the children in pretending to twirl magic lassos.)* Those two words are, "Thank you." Let's practice that. *(Lead the children in saying, "Thank you." Do it a couple of times.)*

That's pretty easy, right? But it's one thing to say, "Thank you." It's another thing to know when to say it. First of all, we can say thank you to God every day for making such a wonderful world full of wonderful people. Let's say, "Thank you!" to God. *(Lead the children in saying, "Thank you.")*

We can say thank you to our families for loving us and taking such good care of us. Let's say thank you to our families." *(Lead the children in saying, "Thank you.")*

Our worship leaders, from the clergy to the musicians to the acolytes, work hard to make worship inspiring for all of us. Let's say thank you to all our worship leaders." *(Lead the children in saying, "Thank you.")*

You know, I'm sure that just about everyone in our congregation has done something for you, maybe without your even knowing it. Let's say thank you to the whole congregation. *(Lead the children in saying, "Thank you.")*

And I know the whole congregation loves having you here to worship with us. You add so much to each service by being exactly who you are. I think the congregation would like to say something to you. *(Lead the congregation in saying, "Thank you.")*

WOW TiMe

You know, we're very lucky. Every moment of every day, someone is doing something for us. Maybe it's a teacher. Maybe it's a parent. Maybe it's a friend. And it's always God. There are so many times when saying those two simple words "thank you" are very powerful. And when you say thank you to someone who has done something for you, it makes that person feel appreciated. And it probably makes that person feel like doing something for someone else. You did a great job today. Thank you.

CLoSiNG

For this children's moment we all, children and adults, sang the words "thank you" to the tune of the popular African-American spiritual, *Amen*. You can sing it a couple of times. I also asked everyone to stand and (yes) clap on the backbeat. Do what works best for your setting.

we need our rest

THEME
We need to take time to rest so that we can get the most out of God's wonderful world.

SCRIPTURE
Exodus 20:8-11 — Remember the Sabbath Day

PREPARE
Provide a blanket and a pillow for your use. I also wore a really long stocking cap, a la Wee Willie Winkie.

WOW TIME
As the children come to the front, fluff the pillow. Then lie down with your head on the pillow and cover yourself up with the blanket. (You could even snuggle with a stuffed animal.) Once all the children are in place, start snoring.

They will either giggle or call loudly to you to wake you up. You can startle a little bit, then settle back down to "sleep" and continue snoring. Milk this as much as you want. It will be a lot of fun for the children, but your comfort level (both physically and dramatically) will determine how long to draw this out. Eventually "wake up" and stretch as you "notice" that all the children are there.

Oh! Is it time for the children's moment already? I must have overslept. I didn't get much sleep last night. [This next part is completely true, so I used it.] I was watching Saturday Night Live last night, and Will Ferrell was on, and he's so funny that I couldn't fall asleep after that. *(Some laughs behind me from the congregation let me know that I wasn't the only one. The children are laughing too, mostly at my ridiculous hat.)* Have you ever had a time when you just couldn't fall asleep, and the next morning you were exhausted? Tap your nose if that's ever happened to you. *(Most of the children tap their noses.)*

It's very important for us to get rest. When we get enough rest we're able to enjoy and appreciate everything so much more. And when we don't get enough rest, everything is a blur. But rest doesn't always mean sleeping. There are lots of ways we can rest our bodies and minds without sleeping. Let's play a game. I'll act out a way we can rest, and you try to figure out what I'm doing.

(Pretend you are sitting and reading a book. Most of the children will recognize what you are doing and call out the answer.)

That's right. I was sitting and reading. And believe me, I was not reading the dictionary. I was reading *The Wind in the Willows*. I love that book, and it always makes me feel good and relaxed. I want you each to think of your favorite book. *(Give them a few moments to think.)* Now I want each of you to imagine reading that book right now. *(Lead the children in pretending to read their favorite books.)*

Let's try another one. *(Cup a hand to one ear and pretend you are listening. Most of the children will understand that you are listening to something. What exactly that something is will depend on which child is telling you.)*

You're right. I was listening to something. I was listening to some violin music by Johann Sebastian Bach. I always feel like I breathe better when I listen to Bach. Everyone take in a deep, gentle, quiet breath and let it out. *(The children do. Some will take a big loud breath. Remind them to make the breath quiet.)*

Now I want you to think of a song or some other piece of music, that makes you feel like that deep, gentle, quiet breath. Everyone continue to take deep, gentle, quiet breaths as you imagine listening to that music. *(Lead the children through the process of doing this by modeling it yourself.)*

There are so many other ways we can rest — a walk in the park, an unhurried meal with the family. We live in a wonderful world. God wants us to make sure we take time to really rest, so that we can get the most out of what God has given us.

CLOSING
Guide the children through the following prayer. Start by saying the entire phrase "Help me slow down, Lord." Do this in one deep, gentle, quiet breath. The next time have the children breathe before the first and second word. Then before the first, second, and third words, and so on until there is a deep, gentle, quiet breath before each word. Resist the temptation to speed this up. It takes time, and that's the point.

(breath) Help me slow down, Lord.
(breath) Help *(breath)* me slow down, Lord.
(breath) Help *(breath)* me *(breath)* slow down, Lord.
(breath) Help *(breath)* me *(breath)* slow *(breath)* down, Lord.
(breath) Help *(breath)* me *(breath)* slow *(breath)* down. *(breath)* Lord.
(breath) Amen. *(breath)* *(breath)* *(breath)*

A Time to Listen

It is important to take time to listen — to God and to each other.

SCRIPTURE
Ecclesiastes 3:7b — A Time to Keep Silence and a Time to Speak

WOW TIME
If you like to play outside, raise your hand. *(Many children, if not all, will raise their hands.)* If you like to sing, use your hands to make moose antlers. *(Many children will make moose antlers.)* If you like to go on a trip with your family, clap your hands three times. *(Many children will clap their hands; some more than four times).* If you like to sit and listen while someone else talks, tap your nose. *(Some children, maybe even more than you might expect, will tap their noses. Many will not.)*

I sometimes have a hard time sitting and listening to someone else. Sometimes I'd rather be busy playing, singing, or going out on some adventure. But it is important to take the time to listen to others. We can learn a lot that way. It helps us get to know and understand people better. And it helps us get the most out of life. Besides, if we didn't take time to stop and listen… we wouldn't be able to… tell knock-knock jokes. Let's try a few.

Knock-knock. *(The children respond, "Who's there?")* Anita. *(The children ask, "Anita who?")* Anita learn some better knock-knock jokes.

The children laugh, though they aren't quite sure why. It's interesting to watch children respond to knock-knock jokes. Most young children don't understand the puns that make up the basis for the humor in most knock-knock jokes. But they love the give-and-take (or speak-and-listen) of the form. For many of them, the laughter at the end is simply part of the form of a good knock-knock joke.

Knock-knock. *(The children respond, "Who's there?")* Little old lady. *(The children ask, "Little old lady, who?")* I didn't know you could yodel. *(The children laugh again.)*

Knock-knock. *(The children respond, "Who's there?")* Boo. *(The children ask, "Boo who?")* Aw, don't cry. *(More laughter.)*

Knock-knock. *(The children respond, "Who's there?")* Thistle. *(The children ask, "Thistle who?")* Thistle be the last knock-knock joke. *(The children laugh. There may also be some playfully sarcastic applause from the congregation that it's your last joke.)*

See? In each knock-knock joke there were important times for you to sit and listen. Otherwise you wouldn't have known how to respond, and the jokes wouldn't have been very funny. But you listened to me some of the time. I listened to you some of the time. And we all laughed. We got the most out of the knock-knock jokes because we took the time to sit and listen to each other."

CLoSiNG

Let's close with an echo prayer. Listen carefully to each line I say. And I will listen as you echo that line. Let us pray. *(Have the children repeat each line after you in this echo prayer.)*

Dear God,
Help us remember,
To take time
To listen —
To listen to others,
And to listen to you.
(Take a few seconds to listen.)
Amen.

BURSTING BALLOONS

THEME
We don't make ourselves bigger by making others feel smaller. We should encourage others.

SCRIPTURE
1 Thessalonians 5:11 — Encourage One Another

PREPARE
Provide two large inflated balloons, one small inflated balloon, a pin, two balloons (not yet inflated), and an inflated balloon for each child. I chose to invest in a small helium tank I got from a party supply store. I inflated the balloons and attached ribbons to each well before the children's moment. I also had a few Mylar® balloons on hand for any children with latex allergies.

WOW TIME
As the children are coming down, hand each of the two large balloons to a minister or other adult who can stand next to you. Hold the smallest of the three balloons in one hand, and the pin concealed in the other.

Who has the smallest balloon? *(The children will answer, "You do.")* I'm going to try to make my balloon bigger. Now I want you to watch my balloon closely. And you might want to cover your ears. Is everyone watching? Here I go. *(Pop one of the big balloons held by an adult helper.)* Did everyone watch my balloon? *(The children will answer, "Yes.")* Did my balloon get any bigger? *(Most of the children will answer, "No.")*

So even though I made his/her balloon pop, it didn't make my balloon any bigger? Hmm, maybe I did something wrong. Let me try that again. Make sure you watch my balloon very carefully. *(Pop the large balloon held by the other adult helper.)* I popped his/her balloon. Did that make my balloon any bigger? *(Most children will answer, "No.")*

You're right. My balloon stayed the same size. When I popped my friends' balloons, not only did my balloon not get any bigger, but now my friends don't have any balloons at all. And that makes me feel kind of sad.

(Take out the balloons that haven't been inflated yet.) But what if I give a balloon to each of my friends? While I do this next part, make sure to

keep watching my balloon. *(Inflate the two balloons and give one to each of the adult helpers. Make sure the balloons are larger than the one you are holding. You may need to set your balloon aside while inflating the other two.)* I inflated two balloons, and gave one to each of my friends. Did my balloon get any bigger? *(Most children will answer, "No.")* Did my balloon get any smaller? *(Most children will answer, "No.")*

Right. My balloon stayed the same size. But you know what? I feel a lot better. Giving my friends balloons feels a lot better than popping them. It feels so good that it doesn't even matter to me if their balloons are a little bit bigger. In fact, I like it so much that I'm going to give each of you a balloon. *(The children cheer enthusiastically.)*

At the end of the worship service, come right to the front of the sanctuary. I will have a balloon for each of you. I even have a few Mylar® balloons for any of you with latex allergies. *(That last part was more for the parents than the children. One of the reasons I wait until the end of the service to hand out balloons is because then the children are more likely to come down with their parents. Many children may not know if they are allergic to latex or not. So having a responsible, knowledgeable adult with them is very helpful. By the way, you may choose to get enough Mylar® balloons for all the children. It costs a little more, but may well be worth it. It really depends on your setting.)*

CLosiNG
Today we'll close with a call-and-response prayer. I will say something different each time and you always respond by saying, "Up." Let us pray.

Whenever I feel small, your love lifts me,	*Children:* **Up.**
Whenever I feel low, your love cheers me,	*Children:* **Up.**
Whenever I feel outnumbered, your love backs me,	*Children:* **Up.**
Whenever I feel worn out, your love wakes me,	*Children:* **Up.**
Whenever I feel empty, your love fills me,	*Children:* **Up.**

THe CoNCReTe BaLLoon
The whole notion of "bursting someone else's balloon" is a great metaphor… for older children and adults. But if I'd left it there, it would have missed the mark with the younger children. Younger children will connect the fact that giving balloons to our friends feels better (and is better) than popping their balloons. Without that very important aspect, this successful children's moment would have been just another well-intentioned, ultimately ineffective, object lesson.

Because we can

THEME
We should do the right thing, not because we have to, but because we can.

SCRIPTURE
Isaiah 1:17 — Learn to Do Good; 1 Thessalonians 5:15 — Seek to Do Good

WOW TIME
Let's imagine that we're at the mall. Come walk with me. *(Lead the children in a "mall walk" around the sanctuary.)* First we're walking by the place at the mall where people go to get a haircut. We look inside and see a kid getting all his hair cut off because the night before, he fell asleep with gum in his hair and it's all stuck. Now, we could all point and laugh at him. There's no law against it. But that would make him feel bad. Instead of pointing and laughing at him, let's smile and wave to him. He looks like he could use a friend right now. *(Lead the children in waving to the imaginary boy getting his hair cut.)* I like it when we do the right thing, not because we have to, but because we can. Okay, let's keep walking.

(Lead the children farther around the sanctuary.) Oh, this is one of the best places in the mall — the food court! Can you smell that? It's the place where they make the cookies. And we're very lucky, because they've just put out some free samples. I LOVE it when they do that. Now we could take all the samples for ourselves if we wanted to. They are free, after all. What should we do? *(Many of the children will say, "We should take one and leave the rest for other people.")* That's a good idea. Let's each just take one and leave the rest for others, not because we have to, but because we can. *(Lead the children in pretending to take a piece of cookie and eat it.)* Mm. That was so yummy. Let's keep walking through the mall.

(Pause) Uh-oh. We see a little girl who looks lost. We could keep walking by if we want. She's not our sister. What should we do? *(Children may respond, "We should help her find her parents.")* That's a good idea. Let's tell our parents. We can stay with her until her parents come, not because we have to but... *(Lead the children to finish the statement,)* ... because we can! And sure enough, here come her parents right now. They give us a big "thank you" and wave to us as they leave. *(Lead the children in waving.)*

Finally, we make our way to the best store in the whole mall — the toy store! We've saved up our allowance and have five dollars. We're here to get a really cool toy. When we get in line we realize we'll have 25 cents left over. That's just enough to put in one of those cool gum ball machines where the giant gum ball goes around and around before finally coming out. I can just taste it.

(Pause) But wait. There's a problem in the line. The kid in front of us is getting a birthday present for his little brother, but he doesn't have enough money. Guess how much he needs? *(Many of the children will guess, "25 cents.")* You guessed it — 25 cents. We'll have 25 cents left over. If we give it to him so he can get the present for his little brother, it means we won't be able to go get a gum ball out of that really cool gum ball machine. What should we do? *(Most of the children will say something like, "Give the boy the 25 cents.")* You know what? *(sigh)* As usual, you're right. Let's give the boy the 25 cents so he can get the present for his little brother, not because we have to, but… *(The children will jump in, "… because we can." Lead the children in pretending to hand the money to the boy.)*

There. We did a lot of very good things today. It feels good doing good things, not because we have to, but… *(The children will say, "… because we can.")*

CLOSING
Let's close with a call-and-response prayer. I will say something different each time, and you respond by saying, "Because we can." Let us pray.

We will be kind to others, not because we have to but…
Children: … **Because we can.**
We will share with others, not because we have to but…
Children: … **Because we can.**
We will help those is need, not because we have to but…
Children: … **Because we can.**

KEEP CLIMBING

THEME
Keep doing what is right, even when it's difficult.

SCRIPTURE
Galatians 6:9 — If We Do Not Give Up; 1 Corinthians 15:58 — In the Lord, Your Labor Is Not in Vain

WOW TIME

I'm going to show you one of my favorite songs. I'm not going to sing it yet. I'm just going to show you. And you're all so smart, I bet you'll guess it in no time. *(Show the motions for* The Itsy Bitsy Spider.*)*

I'm assuming most of you know the motions for The Itsy Bitsy Spider. *But just in case:*

The itsy bitsy spider climbed up the water spout.
(Touch index finger of the right hand to the thumb of the left hand. Then while moving the hands upward, touch the index finger of the left hand to the thumb of the right hand. The other fingers should look like the spider's legs.)

Down came the rain,
(Start with hands up, palms facing downward. Wiggle the fingers as you lower the hands to indicate rain.)

And washed the spider out.
(Move hands away from body, waist-high to indicated a rush of water "washing' the spider away.)

Out came the sun,
(Make a circle with the arms over your head to indicate the sun.)

And dried up all the rain.
(Move hands side-to-side, palms down and waist-high to indicate the rain drying up.)

And the itsy bitsy spider climbed up the spout again.
(Do motions for the first line of the song.)

(Most of the children will call out, "It's The Itsy Bitsy Spider!") That's right, it's *The Itsy Bitsy Spider*. I told you you were smart. Let's all speak the words and do the motions together. *(Lead the children through the words and motions of* The Itsy Bitsy Spider. *Most of them will know it backwards and forwards. But you never know who might be seeing this for the first time.)*

But it never says, "And the Itsy Bitsy Spider made it all the way to the top of the water spout. And when she got there, she got a trophy and a gold medal for making it all the way to the top. And there was a big chocolate cake and in yellow icing was written "Way to Go, Itsy Bitsy Spider. You Did What You Set Out to Do. You Did It! You Did It! You Did It!" *(This is usually followed by laughter from the children.)*

Maybe she makes it all the way to the top of the water spout. But maybe the rain comes and washes her right out again. Do you know why I like *The Itsy Bitsy Spider* so much? *(The children ask, "Why?")* Because she never stops climbing. That water may wash her right down the spout. But she gets right back up, dries herself off, and keeps climbing.

We're not always going to win the race. We're not always going to get first place in the spelling bee. But does that mean we should quit? *(Most children will respond, "No.")*

If we don't get it all right the first time, should we just give up? *(Most children will respond, "No.")* Or, like the Itsy Bitsy Spider, should we keep trying? *(The children will respond, "Yes!")*

Let's all stand up and sing the song together. And this will be our closing for today.

CLOSING
Have the children join you in singing and performing the motions for The Itsy Bitsy Spider.

Look, Listen, Learn

THEME
We can learn so much when we look and when we listen.

SCRIPTURE
Luke 10:38-42 — Mary and Martha

PREPARE
Provide a kazoo and an action figure for yourself. I used an Albert Einstein action figure. (Yes, they make those.)

WOW TIME
How many eyes did God give us? *(The children will answer, "Two.")* Let's blink our eyes five times. *(Count "1-2-3-4-5" as you blink with the children five times.)*

How many ears did God give us? *(The children will answer, "Two.")* Let's wiggle our ears six times. *(Count "1-2-3-4-5-6" as you and the children use your fingers to make your ears wiggle six times. Maybe a child can wiggle his or her ears without using hands. Cool!)*

God gave us two eyes for looking and two ears for listening so we can learn everything. It's important to keep our eyes and ears in shape so we'll learn all we possibly can.

Let's play a game. Everybody stand up. *(Wait for the children to stand. It won't take long. Hold up the action figure.)* I want you to use your eyes and look carefully at the action figure I'm holding. Any time I move part of the action figure, I want you to move that same part of your body. For example, if I raise this arm... *(Raise one of the action figure's arms)...* you raise that same arm. Got it? Here we go.

Move the action figure in any number of ways. Raise one arm. Raise both arms. Lower an arm. Raise one leg. Make the action figure hop. Make it do a complete turn. The kids will love this.

Great watching! You really used your eyes well. We also have two ears for listening. I'm going to play this kazoo, and I want you to use your ears to listen. When you hear me playing the kazoo, I want you to flap your arms and buzz like bees. But as soon as I stop playing, you have to freeze in place. Here we go.

Play and stop several times, as the children play along. Once they catch on, get trickier — play only a very short passage before stopping, or even play a very long one before stopping. Break up the rhythm so that it's unpredictable.

Great listening! You really used your ears well. When our eyes are in shape for looking, and our ears are in shape for listening, we are ready to learn all about God and God's love for us. And guess what? God gave us two eyes, and two ears. But how many mouths do we have? *(The children will answer, "One.")*

Hmm. One mouth. You're right. Do you think maybe we should look and listen twice as much as we talk?" *(You may get some disagreement from some of the children on this. That's okay. Best to leave that one hanging.)*

Closing
Invite the children to repeat after you each line of this short prayer.

Dear God,
Thank you for our eyes.
Thank you for our ears.
Thank you for our mouths.
Please help us know
When to open what.
Amen.

Adapting
Perhaps you have a child that is vision- or hearing-impaired. Can't they learn just as much about God's love? Certainly! Consider adapting this children's moment to include our two hands which can be used to read Braille or sign. Do what works best for your situation.

Servant Safari

THEME
Anyone can be a servant who helps God and God's people.

SCRIPTURE
Ephesians 4:11-12 — Equipping the Saints for the Work of Ministry

PREPARE
Provide a book, a couple of Band-Aids®, and a hammer. Fold a blank piece of paper (8 ½ x 11 inches) into thirds. On one third make a simple line drawing of a book. On one third make a simple line drawing of a couple of Band-Aids®. On the final third make a simple line drawing of a hammer. On the back of the sheet of paper, in big letters that take up the entire sheet, write the words All of Us. *If you don't fancy yourself the best artist in the world, you can either label the pictures, or have someone else draw them for you.*

Before the worship service, you need to have three willing helpers:

1. *A Sunday school teacher who can hold the book.*
2. *A nurse, doctor, or other healer who can hold the Band-Aids®.*
3. *A person who has worked on a Habitat for Humanity® house, or perhaps gone on a mission trip, who can hold the hammer.*

Inform your adult helpers that they will need to stand when their particular role of service has been mentioned during the children's moment.

WOW TIME
Today we are going on a Servant Safari. We are going to look for special people who serve God and God's people. I have a guidebook that will help us find the servants. *(The guidebook is the sheet of paper folded in thirds. Make sue to hold it so that the pictures are visible, but the words on the back are concealed.)* Don't forget to put on your mosquito spray. *(Lead the children in pretending to spray on mosquito repellent.)* Make sure you have your binoculars ready. *(Lead the children in pretending to put binoculars around your neck.)*

(Hold up the guidebook to show the picture of the book.) What is this? *(The children will say, "A book.")* Okay. Let's look out in the wild congregation. Use you binoculars to see if you can find the book. *(Lead the children in*

searching the congregation with your pretend binoculars. The adult helper with the book should hold it up at this time. The children will spot the book fairly quickly, and tell you about it.)

Aha! You spotted the book. Great work! (Go out into the congregation where the adult helper is holding the book. Invite the helper to stand up. Then say,) You are holding a book. Are you a servant of God? (The volunteer will answer, "Yes I am." Ask,) How do you serve? (The volunteer will answer, "I serve by teaching Sunday school.")

(Turn to the children.) Hey, we found a servant. S/he teaches Sunday school. Everybody get out your cameras and take a picture. (Lead the children in pretending to take pictures of the teacher. Invite the volunteer to sit down as you go back to the children.)

(Show the picture of the adhesive bandages.) What are these? (Most of the children will say, "Band-Aids®.") Get your binoculars ready and see if you can spot the Band-Aids®. (Lead the children in searching the congregation. The adult helper with the Band-Aids® will hold them up. The children will indicate when they have spotted the Band-Aids®.) Yes! There they are. Way to go!

(Go out into the congregation where the adult helper is holding the Band-Aids®. Invite the helper to stand up. Then say,) You are holding Band-Aids®. Are you a servant of God? (The volunteer will answer, "Yes. I help people when they are hurt. I try to make them feel better.")

(Tell the children,) We found another servant. S/he is a healer. Get those cameras back out and take some more pictures. (Lead the children in pretending to take pictures of the healer. Invite the volunteer to sit down as you go back to the children.)

(Show the picture of the hammer.) What is this? (The children will answer, "It's a hammer.") Get your binoculars ready and see if you can find a hammer. (Lead the children in searching the congregation. The adult helper with the hammer should hold it up now. The children will spot the hammer immediately and let you know.) You did it again! You found the hammer.

(Go out into the congregation where the adult helper is holding the hammer. Invite the helper to stand up. Then say,) You are holding a hammer. Are you a servant of God? (The volunteer will answer, "Yes. I'm a servant of God. I worked to help build a house for a family in need.")

(Tell the children,) We found another servant. S/he is a builder. Get out your cameras and take more pictures. *(Lead the children in pretending to take pictures of the builder. Invite the volunteer to sit down as you go back to the children.)*

We found three different servants on our Servant Safari. Not bad. *(Look at the guidebook for a second. Look slightly puzzled. Then turn it over to see the writing on the other side. Then say,)* You know what? I was holding this guidebook upside down the whole time. Now I know where we can find a whole bunch of servants. *(Hold the paper so the children can read it.)* What does that say? *(Guide the children as they read, "All of Us.")* That's right. All of us can be servants of God. All of us can be teachers who help others learn about God's love. All of us can be healers who help others feel better. All of us can be builders who make life better for those in need. There's no end to the ways we can all be servants. Okay, get your cameras ready. We're about to see a WHOLE BUNCH of servants. Everyone in this room — congregation, clergy, musicians, grown-ups, children — if you can be a servant of God, stand up.

(Everyone stands up.) Okay, get your cameras out. And let's take pictures of all the servants in here. *(Let everyone pretend to take pictures for a few seconds. Then invite all to sit down.)* All of us are servants of God. This has been a wonderful safari!

CLꙩSiNG
Invite the children to repeat after you each line of the following prayer-poem.

Each day, God gives us the chance
To love and serve each other;
And everyone we meet can be
A sister or a brother.

God only wants what's best for us.
God blesses as we live,
And gives us power to teach and help,
To build up and to give.
Amen.

Enough to Share

THEME

God created a world full of abundance. It's up to us to share it.

SCRIPTURE

John 6:1-13 — Feeding the Five Thousand

PREPARE

Place five sheets of white paper and two small bundles of crayons in a basket. You may need to adjust the size of the sheets and the bundles of crayons according to the size of the group. The idea is to have more children than sheets and crayons. Before the service, place the basket near where the children gather for the children's moment.

WOW TIME

I would like for each of us to be able to make a picture of your favorite food. But I don't think we have enough materials for everyone to make a picture. Does anybody know where we can find some things to help us make our pictures? *(Hopefully the children will have found the basket by now. If not, nudge them a little until they do.)*

Oh good, you found the basket. I knew I put it down here before the service. I just couldn't remember where. Let's see what we have inside the basket. We have paper. Let's see if we have enough. 1-2-3-4-5, we only have five sheets of paper. And we have a lot more than five people here today. We also have crayons. Let's count how many bundles of crayons we have. 1-2, we only have two bundles of crayons. This isn't enough for everyone. What can we do?" *(Give the children some time to come up with the answer themselves. If they struggle, offer a leading question, such as, "How could I take this one piece of paper and turn it into two pieces?" Most of the children will have a solution.)*

So if I tear these five big pieces of paper into several smaller pieces, everyone can have some paper? *(The children will answer, "Yes.")* And if we break these crayons into many smaller crayons, everyone will have something to color with? *(The children will answer, "Yes.")*

I think that's a great idea. I'll tear the paper. I need a few volunteers to help me break the crayons into smaller ones. I'm going to choose the three quietest hands I can find. *(Choose three quiet volunteers to break up the* crayons while you tear the paper into smaller pieces. Have the volunteers use the basket to put the smaller crayon pieces in.)

(While this is being done, you can sing the first verse of Pass It On or Jesus Loves Me with the other children. Then have the volunteers help you distribute a small crayon and small sheet of paper to each child. If you find that you run out of paper or crayons, simply break a small piece into two smaller ones. Try to set it up in such a way that there is some paper and crayons left over. Put the leftovers in the basket.)

Everybody got a piece of paper, and everybody got a crayon. It may not have been exactly what we expected, but there was enough for everybody. And look. (Show the basket.) There was even some left over. Don't forget to make a picture of your favorite food. And because we shared with each other, we can all make our pictures, and no one is left out.

CLOSING
Have the children repeat after you each line of the following prayer-poem.

Sometimes the things we have to do
Aren't easy, quick, or fun.
But God will be there at the start,
And when our task is done.

God fills our lives with love and hope,
But doesn't stop right there;
God always gives us extra,
So we'll have enough to share.
Amen.

Lost and Found

Theme
God loves each one of us very much. If even one of us feels lost or alone, that matters to God.

Scripture
Luke 15:3-7 — The Parable of the Lost Sheep; Luke 15:8-10 — The Parable of the Lost Coin.

Prepare
Put two "childhood" items, such as a baseball and a toy, in a paper bag. Before the worship service, choose an adult volunteer to sit in the congregation and hold a stuffed animal or blanket.

Wow Time
(Hold up the paper bag.) I want to show you some of my favorite things. They're here in this bag. *(Reach into the bag and pull out the baseball. Milk this part a little. Really look like you're fishing around in the bag before you find something. It will build some excitement.)* Here is my baseball. I love baseball. I love playing it. I love watching it. When I was younger I would play catch in the backyard with my dad every evening. *(Set the baseball aside.)*

Let's see what else is in here. *(Fish around and pull out the toy. In my case it was a slinky I'd used in a previous children's moment.)* This is my slinky. It's fun to try and make it walk. I would stack up all my books to make steps and see if I could get the slinky to walk all the way down. *(Play with the slinky in your hands for a few seconds. Then set it aside.)*

(Reach back into the bag as you say,) But what I really want to show you is… *(You can't find it. The bag is empty.)* Where is Darwin?

Darwin is a puppet I made myself. I actually made him out of objects from a lost-and-found box. That's why I thought to use him for this children's moment. Later some of the adults shared that they thought I was just trying to be funny by having the children "search for Darwin" in church. Nope. It was just coincidence — funny, but a coincidence.

(Some children may ask, "What's Darwin?") Darwin is a puppet I made myself. *(Feel free to substitute a stuffed animal, blanket, or whatever works for*

you.) He's very special to me. Well, maybe we should just continue with the children's moment.

(Pause for a few seconds, looking distracted. Then say,) You know what? I just can't concentrate. Darwin is really important to me. I need to look for him. *(Pause)* Do you think you can come help me find him? *(The children will answer, "Yes.")*

That's great. I really appreciate it. Follow me and we'll go around the sanctuary looking for him. Keep your eyes open. You'll know him when you see him. He looks like a Darwin. *(Lead the children around the sanctuary. When you and the children are about halfway around, have your adult helper start to raise the stuffed animal/blanket. Before long the children will start to spot Darwin. Some will say, "There he is!")*

Go over to the volunteer and get Darwin. Thank the volunteer for taking such good care of him. Then lead the children back to where they normally gather for the children's moment.

Thank you so much for helping me to find Darwin. I couldn't have done it without you. And now I feel so much better. Did you know that God loves each one of us way, way more than I love Darwin? No matter how sad, lost, or alone we feel sometimes, God always wants to bring us back to a place where we feel loved. And just like you helped me find Darwin, we can all help God. If we see someone who looks lonely or sad, we can help that person feel better by being kind and friendly. Will you help God look for people that need our help? *(The children answer, "Yes.")* That's wonderful. And thanks again for helping me find Darwin.

CLOSING
Have the children repeat after you each line of the following prayer.

Loving God,
Sometimes I might feel lost,
But I know I'm never alone,
Because you are always there
To love me,
And hold me,
And guide me safely home.
Amen.

WHEN HENRY DIED

THEME
When a loved one, such as a friend, a family member, or a pet, dies, it means their body stops working. But love does not. Love never ends.

SCRIPTURE
1 Corinthians 13:4-8a — Love never ends.

OFF THE MARK
This is a difficult children's moment. Every All Saint's Sunday, I try to explore the concept of death and dying with the children. One year I used a piece of candy and explained that the inside was the good, sweet part that we loved, and that the wrapper was like the body. The following year I used the image of a balloon that had run out of air. The balloon itself was empty, but the air was still all around us. I got great responses from many of the adults. But I never felt like I reached the children. These are examples of two object lessons that require abstract thinking to interpret the metaphors. If the goal of a children's moment is to bring children to a better understanding of God's love, then I was off the mark.

So after two years of feeling disappointed in my lack of connection with the children on this subject, I did a lot of searching. What I found was that virtually all experts agree the best way to talk with children about death and dying is to actually talk with them about death and dying. Euphemisms often confuse children, especially younger ones. To tell a child that someone "went away" leaves the possibility that he or she might come back. To say that someone "went to sleep for a long time" leaves the possibility that he or she might wake up. It also can make children afraid of falling asleep. "What if I fall asleep tonight, and don't wake up?" The best advice I got was to be gentle and honest. And if I was asked a question that I couldn't answer, saying "I don't know" is always an option.

This children's moment doesn't have a lot of pop or pizzazz — no candy wrappers or balloons. It is a simple, true story about the first time I dealt with the death of something I loved — my pet hamster, Henry.

Obviously this is a sensitive subject and it is important to communicate with the parents in advance that you will be dealing with the subject of death. A note in the worship bulletin will help. I also like to put book recommendations in the bulletin. Here are a few I think work very well:

When a Pet Dies by Fred Rogers; Putnam Juvenile, 1998.

The Tenth Good Thing About Barney by Judith Viorst; Aladdin, 1987.

The Fall of Freddie the Leaf by Leo Buscaglia, Ph.D.; Slack Incorporated, 1982.

WOW Time

Do any of you have pets? *(Many children will say, "Yes.")* Raise your hand if you have a dog. *(Some children will raise their hands.)* Raise your hand if you have a cat. *(Some children will raise their hands, including some who raised their hands already).* Raise your hand if you have a fish. *(Some children will raise their hands.)* Raise your hand if you have a pet that I haven't named yet. *(Some children will raise their hands, and even try to tell you what that pet is. If time allows, and you have an intimate enough group, you might invite each child to tell you what kind of pet he or she has.)*

When I was seven years old, I got a hamster for my birthday. I named him Henry. I fed him every day, and cleaned his cage once a week. If I didn't clean his cage, it would smell pretty bad. Sometimes I held him and stroked his soft fur. My favorite thing to do was put him in his exercise ball and watch him roll all around the house.

One morning I went to look at Henry, but he wasn't moving. Usually when he would lie down, he was sleeping and his chest would go in and out while he breathed. But he wasn't doing that. So I ran to get my dad. He came in, took Henry out of his cage, and held him very gently. Then my dad told me that Henry had died.

I thought about that for a second. Then I remembered a time when Henry was sick. We took him to the animal hospital and they gave him some medicine to make him feel better. "Can we take Henry to the animal hospital?" I asked. My dad answered, "When someone dies, it means their body stops working. Even if we took Henry to the animal hospital, they wouldn't be able to make his body work again."

I thought some more. Then I asked, "Does that mean I won't be able to play with Henry anymore?" My dad answered, "Yes son, that's what it means. I'm sorry." That made me sad, and I cried. I had never had a pet that died, and I didn't know what to do. My dad said that we could bury him in the backyard. The two of us chose a place near a mulberry tree.

My dad dug a deep hole. We put Henry in a little shoebox, and I put the box in the hole. Then my dad covered the box by filling the hole with dirt. That made me sad, too. My dad knelt down beside me and said, "Son, I'm sorry Henry died. But did you know that love doesn't die?" I wasn't sure what that meant. I said, "But Dad, we buried Henry. And I won't be able to play with him anymore." My dad asked, "But do you still love Henry?" "Yes," I responded, "I still love him." "See? You can't bury love. Love doesn't end."

I had to think about that for a while. Something about that made me feel a little bit better, but I wasn't sure why. Then my dad asked me to do something — think of my three favorite memories about Henry.

I thought and I thought. "Well," I said, "one of my favorite memories about Henry was the day I got him. It felt special to have a pet I took care of by myself." "That's a good memory," said my dad. "You always took great care of Henry."

I thought some more. Then I said, "I remember how his fur feels. When I petted him, it made me feel warm and relaxed." My dad answered, "That's another great memory. Henry loved it when you would pet him."

Then I thought some more, and another memory came to me. I said, "I always liked watching Henry run around the house in his exercise ball." The thought of his little feet going so fast in that big ball made me giggle. I didn't know if it was okay for me to laugh. Was I supposed to just be sad? "You go ahead and laugh," my dad said. "All those wonderful memories you have of Henry mean your love for him is still alive. Love doesn't die."

I still felt a little sad. I still missed Henry. But I also had wonderful memories of Henry, and I still felt love for him. And that made me feel better.

CLOSING

Have the children repeat after you each line of the following prayer.

Trees may fall,	But Love lives forever —
But Faith stands.	Their love lives forever.
Flowers may fade,	Our love lives forever.
But Hope lasts.	God's love lives forever.
Loved ones may die,	Amen.

FOLLOW UP

If your children go to Sunday school, or some other place away from the sanctuary after children's moments, offer opportunities for the conversation to continue. Children could ask questions, pray, journal, or even participate in an art project as a form of expression based on the subject. Do what you think is appropriate for your setting.

Talents

THEME
Each of us has talents we can use to serve God and God's people.

SCRIPTURE
Matthew 25:14-30 — The Parable of the Talents

WOW TIME

(Invite the children to stand up.) How many of you are singers? *(Most, if not all, of the children will raise their hands.)* How many of you are readers? *(Most of the children will raise their hands.)*

If you are a painter, pretend to paint a picture. *(Most of the children will paint enthusiastically.)* If you are very strong, flex your muscles. *(The children will flex their muscles.)*

If you are good with animals, pretend to rock a puppy in your arms. *(Most of the children will pretend to rock a puppy. Some will want a kitten. That's fine.)*

If you are a writer, pretend to write a story. *(The children will pretend to write.)* If you are a dancer, dance in place. *(Most of the children will dance.)*

Wow, you sure are a talented bunch. God gave us talents so that we could serve God's people and make the world a better place. Just think of all the ways you can use your talents. You can:

Sing in a choir;
Read to a little brother or sister;
Paint a picture for a grandparent;
Work in the yard;
Take care of a pet;
Write a letter to someone in the hospital;
Or give a dance recital for your family in the living room.

There are so many ways we can use our talents. Some people bury their talents deep inside, and forget that they even have them. But we all have talents. We all can serve God. And we all can make the world a better place by using the talents that God gave us.

CLOSING

Invite the children to repeat after you each line of the following prayer-poem.

I can love and serve the Lord
In many different ways;
I can pray a silent prayer,
Or shout my thanks and praise.

I can dance and leap and play,
Or sing a simple song.
God likes it when I serve with love,
For love is never wrong.
Amen.

I CONFESS

For years I thought this parable was about burying talents, as in abilities. I had no idea there was such a thing as a coin called a "talent." I always thought it was poetically symbolic — the notion of burying an ability, rather than developing it to the fullest. Honestly, I'm still a little partial to my misunderstanding of this parable.

BY THE WAY

I LOVE this children's moment. When I ask the children "Who is a dancer?" or "Who is a painter?" all their hands go up. They haven't yet learned (been told) that they can't do something. And the boys dance. And the girls have big muscles. One of the most important things I can do is keep them thinking, and believing, this way as long as possible.

THE Nativity
(A Series)

General Theme
The birth story of Jesus.

Scripture
Luke 2:1-20 — The Birth of Jesus, including the Angels and Shepherds.

Prepare
For this series of children's moments, you will need a nativity set that can be safely handled by children. Wrap each figure individually. Different figures will be unwrapped by a child each week, and placed on the altar or some other prominent spot in the worship space. Over the course of several weeks, the entire nativity scene will be built. I decorated a few boxes which I used each time. I wrapped the figures in tissue paper, and put into the boxes only those figures I would need for that week's children's moment.

Mary and Joseph
(First Sunday in Advent)

Specific Theme
Mary and Joseph were called to take care of the baby Jesus, and they did.

Prepare
Wrap the Mary and Joseph figures in advance. Have the words to the first verse of O Little Town of Bethlehem printed in the bulletin or visible on projection screens.

Wow Time
Today is a very special day — it's the first Sunday in Advent. Advent is a season when we get ready for a very special day. What day is that? *(The children, already on pins and needles, say, "Christmas!")* That's right, in only a few weeks, it will be Christmas. Are you so excited you can't stand it? *(The children respond, "Yes!")*

I know it's a little early, but I have a couple of presents that need unwrapping. Do I have two quiet volunteers who would like to open the present for us today? I'll pick the quietest hands I can find.

During the course of this series, allow as many children to unwrap the figures as possible. Select children and allow them to unwrap the figures. Invite the children to hold the figures for the others to see.

Does anyone know who these two people are? *(Most children will say, "Mary and Joseph." They might all know who Mary is, and by association recognize Joseph. Otherwise Joseph might look like one of the shepherds. Poor, second-fiddle Joseph.)* That's right. This is Mary and Joseph. They had a very important job — to take care of baby… *(Allow the children to finish, "Jesus.")* That was a big responsibility to take care of such a special baby. But when God gave them the Good News, they said, "Yes. We will take care of your special son."

Invite the children who unwrapped the figures of Mary and Joseph to put them either on the altar or some other prominent place in the sanctuary where all can see.

Let's imagine we are Mary and Joseph making the long journey to Bethlehem all those years ago. *(Invite the children to stand with you and walk slowly and steadily.)* Now let's imagine we finally see the little town of Bethlehem. And we know that is where the baby Jesus will be born.

Lead the children in singing the first verse of O Little Town of Bethlehem. *Invite the congregation to join in.*

O little town of Bethlehem, how still we see thee lie
Above thy deep and dreamless sleep, the silent stars go by.
Yet in thy dark streets shineth the everlasting light.
The hopes and fears of all the years are met in thee tonight.

CLOSiNG
Invite the children to repeat after you each line of the following prayer.

Dear God,
Thank you for Mary and Joseph.
Taking care of baby Jesus
Would be a lot of work,
But when you called them,
They said, "Yes."
Amen.

THE AniMaLS
(SeCoND SUNDaY in ADVeNT)

SPECiFiC THEME
Jesus' first days on earth were in a humble stable.

PREPARE
Wrap the cow, donkey, and even the sheep figures in advance. Actually, the donkey could be grouped with Mary and Joseph, while the sheep could be grouped with the shepherds. But I kind of like having all the animals grouped together, except for the camel. The camel really does go better with the wise men. Once again, if you wrap them separately, it allows more children to unwrap the figures. And don't forget to make sure Mary and Joseph are in the same spot they were the previous Sunday. Many churches have weddings on Saturday afternoon and evening, and the figures might get moved. Have the words to the first verse of Away in a Manger *printed in the bulletin or visible on the projection screens.*

WOW TiME
Today is a very special day — it's the second Sunday in Advent. Last week we talked about Advent as a season for preparing for what special day? *(The children respond, "Christmas!")* Last week we opened a present. Do you remember who was inside? *(Most of the children will answer, "Mary and Joseph.")* Mary and Joseph, that's right. *(Point out Mary and Joseph. That way any children who had to miss the first Sunday of Advent, which can happen a lot, especially when the first Sunday of Advent is right after Thanksgiving, won't feel so left out.)*

This week we have more presents that need to be opened. I'm going to pick the quietest hands I can find to open the presents for us. *(Choose children to come open the presents. Invite the children to hold the nativity figures for all the children to see.)* What do we have here? *(The children will answer, "A cow. "A donkey." "Sheep!" and all at the same time.)*

We have a lot of animals here. We have a cow, and a donkey, and even some sheep. What sound does a cow make? *(The children will moo.)* What sound does a donkey make? *(The children will hee-haw.)* What sound does a sheep make? *(The children will baa.)* Okay, everybody pick your favorite and let's all make animal sounds together. Ready? 1-2-3, go! *(Allow the children to make whichever animal sound they choose. This will be fun… and loud.)*

I love reading about animals in the Bible. They were made during creation, even before people. They rode on Noah's ark. And they were the first to share their home with Jesus. I think it's amazing that Jesus was so special, but he wasn't born in a big palace or a nice hospital. He was born in a humble stable, among the animals. *(Invite the children holding the figures to place them next to Mary and Joseph in the prominent place.)*

CLoSiNG

Let's close by standing up and singing the first verse of *Away in a Manger*. And as we sing, let's pretend to rock the baby Jesus. *(Lead the children in singing as they pretend to rock the baby. Invite the congregation to sing as well.)*

Away in a manger, no crib for a bed,
The little lord Jesus laid down his sweet head.
The stars in the sky look down where he lay.
The little lord Jesus, asleep on the hay.

BaBY JeSUS
(THiRD SUnDaY in aDVent)

SpeCifiC THeMe
Jesus was a child who lived and laughed and cried just like all of us.

pRePaRe
Wrap the baby Jesus figure in advance. Each week of this series, make sure the figures which have already been unwrapped are still in place. Have the words to the first verse of Joy to the World *printed in the bulletin or visible on the projection screens.*

W⦿W TiMe
Today is a very special day — it's the third Sunday in Advent. And Advent is a season about preparing for… *(Allow the children to complete the sentence, "Christmas!")* Christmas is getting closer. And Christmas is the day we celebrate the birth of… *(Allow the children to complete the sentence, "Jesus!")*

Jesus, that's right. Last week we opened a present. Do you remember what was inside? *(Allow the children to answer, "A cow." "A donkey." "A sheep." or "The animals.")* The animals. Good job. And what was in the present the week before that? *(Allow the children to answer, "Mary and Joseph.")* Right, Mary and Joseph. Can you find Mary, Joseph, and the animals in here right now? *(Allow the children to point, say, or otherwise show where those figures are in the worship space.)*

I have another present today. And I'm going to pick the quietest hand I can find to open it for us. *(Select a child volunteer and have him or her open the present.)* Who is this? *(Most of the children will answer, "Baby Jesus.")* Well done! It's the baby Jesus. I love how we celebrate Jesus' birthday by remembering that he was a baby. We certainly don't celebrate Abraham Lincoln's birthday by thinking about little baby Lincoln, do we? But it's important to remember that Jesus was more than a teacher, a leader, or a savior. He was a kid just like you.

How many of you have ever fallen down and skinned your knee? *(Most of the children will raise their hands.)* That probably happened to Jesus, too. How many of you have ever had to eat something you really didn't like? *(Lots of hands will go up fast for this one.)* Jesus had to do that, too. How many of you have ever laughed at something so hard, you could barely breathe? *(Most of the children will raise their hands.)* That probably happened to Jesus, too. Jesus was a kid, just like you. And when he grew up, he never forgot what it was like to be a kid. And he made sure his followers knew how special children were. And that's good news.

(Invite the child holding the baby Jesus to place it with the other Nativity figures.) Let's all stand up and sing *Joy to the World* to celebrate the birth of Jesus. *(Lead the children in singing the first verse of* Joy to the World. *Invite the congregation to join in.)*

Joy to the world, the Lord is come.
Let earth receive her king.
Let every heart prepare him room,
And heaven and nature sing,
And heaven and nature sing,
And heaven, and heaven and nature sing.

CLOSING
Invite the children to listen as you offer the following prayer.

In the darkness, you said, "Let there be light,"
And there was light.
In the desert, you said, "Let there be life,"
And water sprang forth from the dry ground.
In our distress, you said, "Let there be love,"
And a child was born in a stable in Bethlehem.

We praise you for your gifts of light,
Life, and love;
And we thank you for your greatest gift –
The gift of you.
Amen.

BY THE WAY
This was one of the most touching, beautiful worship moments of my life. When we did this children's moment at our church, one of our most physically active boys was the one who got to hold the baby Jesus figure. He handled it so gently. And when he took it over to the altar to put it with the other figures, he held it as if it were a real baby. I get a little lump in my throat just writing about it.

ANGELS • SHEPHERDS
(FOURTH SUNDAY in ADVENT)

SPECIFIC THEME
Shepherds were the first people to hear the good news of Jesus' birth.

PREPARE
Wrap the shepherd and angel figures in advance. There may be only one of each, or several, depending on your nativity set. Make sure the figures from the three previous weeks are still in place in the worship space. Have the words to the first verse of The First Noel *printed in the bulletin or visible on the projection screens.*

WOW TIME
Let's look at our nativity scene. So far we have Mary, Joseph, a cow, a donkey, a sheep, and of course, baby Jesus. But we have more to add. It's the fourth Sunday in Advent and there are more presents we need to unwrap. As always, I'm going to choose the quietest hands to unwrap the presents for us. *(Choose children to unwrap the figures of the shepherd and the angel.)* Today we have a shepherd and an angel. Which one's the angel? *(Most children will answer, "The one with the wings.")* Oh. And which one's the shepherd? *(Some will say, "The other one," or "The one with the beard.")* You know? I think you're right. *(Invite the children holding the figures to place them with the others in the nativity scene.)*

Let's all stand up and imagine we're shepherds out in a field watching over our flock of sheep at night. We have twelve sheep. Let's count them. *(Lead the children in counting twelve imaginary sheep. As you count, appear to get sleepier. Have the counting get slower. Yawn.)* Counting sheep at night always makes me sleepy. Let's all imagine we're getting sleepy. Our eyes are getting droopy… and we feel like we might… drift… to… zzzz. *(Go through the actions of getting sleepier. Then lead the children in pretending to be asleep.)*

SUDDENLY! *(This wakes them up.)* An angel of the Lord comes and tells us the good news that Jesus is born. The angel tells us where we can find him and his family. So we hurry to Bethlehem as fast as our little shepherd legs can get us there. *(Have the children run in place.)* And when we get there, we see the stable, and we know we have to be very quiet because the baby might be sleeping, and we don't want to wake him up. *(Have the children tip-toe.)*

We see the baby Jesus, and he looks so sweet. And we feel very proud. We're just simple, poor shepherds. But of all the people in the whole world, we are the very first to see the baby Jesus, because Jesus didn't come for just the rich and powerful. He came for everyone.

Let's celebrate the good news by singing *The First Noel*. (*Lead the children in singing the first verse of* The First Noel. *Invite the congregation to join in.*)

The First Noel, the angel did say
Was to certain poor shepherds in fields as they lay.
In fields where they lay keeping their sheep
On a cold winter's night that was so deep.
Noel, noel, noel, noel,
Born is the king of Israel.

CLOSING

Invite the children to listen as you offer the following prayer.

Gracious God,
You sent your son Jesus
To teach us of your love.
He was born in a stable,
And raised as a humble carpenter's son.
Those around him, who didn't know him better,
Might even have thought he was ordinary.
Please help us be open to your love
And the promise that, in your hands,
The ordinary can be extraordinary.
Amen.

GiFT CaRDS
(EPiPHanY SunDaY)

THeMe
Giving; Christmas; Epiphany

SCRiPTURe
Matthew 2:1-12 — The Visit of the Wise Men

PREPaRe
Using index cards, make a "gift card" for each child. The gift cards should read:
> *10 friendly waves*
> *5 hugs for a family member or friend*
> *3 phone calls to relatives just to say "I love you"*

You could add others, such as 2 times helping parents with the chores, and so forth.

WOW TiMe

Well, Christmas has come and gone, and it is now officially "Gift Card Season." People everywhere go out to spend the gift cards they got for Christmas. I have a special surprise today. I wanted to make sure that you didn't get left out of all the excitement. So I have a gift card for each one of you! *(Cheers from the children.)* As I pass out these gift cards to each of you, let's sing the first verse of *Joy to the World*.

(Sing the first verse of Joy to the World, *or whatever Christmas hymn you feel is appropriate, such as* Away in a Manger *or* O Come All Ye Faithful. *Singing a song while handing something out to each child keeps everyone more focused.)*

You will notice that your gift cards have some interesting items. These aren't gifts that you get. They're gifts for you to give. I love the Christmas season, and I always wish it would last longer, don't you? *(The children agree wholeheartedly.)*

Well, one of the best ways to make the true spirit of Christmas last, is to keep giving. But we don't have to give away stuff, to keep the spirit of Christmas alive! The best gifts are things you can do for others, like telling a family member that you love them, or giving a friend a hug. Let's spend one of the items on your cards. How about if we all give a big friendly wave to all the grown-ups in the congregation? *(The children smile and wave. The grown-ups smile even bigger and wave back.)*

See there? We're ALL keeping the Christmas spirit alive. Now, don't worry if you spend all the items on your card. I have plenty more where that came from. Besides, these cards are completely worthless, unless we spend them.

CLOSING

Have the children repeat after you each line of the following poem by Christina Rossetti.

What can I give him,
Poor as I am?
If I were a shepherd,
I would bring a lamb.

If I were a Wise Man,
I would do my part;
Yet what I can I give him;
Give my heart.
Amen.

BY THE WAY

I talked to a few parents whose children really thought hard about how they were going to spend their gift cards.

Peace in Many Languages

THEME
We don't have to come from the same country, or speak the same language, to understand that God wants us to live in love and peace with one another.

SCRIPTURE
Acts 2:1-11 — The Coming of the Holy Spirit (Pentecost)

PREPARE
Using several sheets of white cardstock and a marker, write the word "peace" in a different language on each sheet. Here are some examples:

Spanish — **paz** *(PAHS)*
Hebrew — **shalom** *(shah-LOHM)*
Hawaiian — **malu** *(MAH-loo)*
Swahili – **amani** *(ah-MAH-nee)*
Russian – **mir** *(MEER)*
Japanese – **heiwa** *(HEY-wah)*

If you have members of your church family that speak other languages, including sign language, by all means invite them to share how they say "peace." It's also a good idea to have all the examples of "peace" in many languages printed in the bulletin or visible on the projection screens. That way the entire congregation can participate.

WOW TIME
(Hold up the card of the word paz.*)* Paz. This is how to say peace in Spanish. Let's all say it together. *(Lead the children in saying, "Paz.")*

Do the same for all the other words for peace. Make sure all the children can see each word, and that you pronounce each one slowly, and clearly. Also, make sure the children know the language for each example.

You can have the children say the word to the congregation. Then have the congregation say it back to the children.

Those are just a few of the ways we can say peace in different languages. Now here's what I want you to do — think about your favorite way to say peace. Then when I say "Go," I want you to turn to you neighbor and say peace in whatever language you chose. Then say it to another neighbor, and then another. And this includes everyone in the entire congregation. You are all invited. Ready? Go!

Have everyone exchange the peace in many languages. You can direct the congregation to find the words for peace in the bulletin or on the projection screens.

Let the passing of the peace take some time. I've visited churches where the passing of the peace was a warm, heartfelt moment in the service. And I've visited churches where it seemed like just one more thing to check off of the worship "to do" list. The effect you should get is a swirl of sound, in many languages.

Did you hear that? What a sound—so many people speaking so many different languages! But it all meant the same thing. What was it? *(Allow the children to respond, "Peace.")*

See? We don't all have to live in the same country, or speak the same language to understand that God wants us to love each other and live in peace.

CLOSiNG

Let's close with a prayer for peace. I will say *peace* in a different language each time, and you respond by saying, "A prayer for peace." Let us pray.

Paz.
Children: **A prayer for peace.**
Shalom.
Children: **A prayer for peace.**
Malu.
Children: **A prayer for peace.**
Amani
Children: **A prayer for peace.**
Mir.
Children: **A prayer for peace.**
Heiwa.
Children: **A prayer for peace.**
Amen.

Treasure Hunt

THEME
Our relationships with God and each other are more important than stuff.

SCRIPTURE
Matthew 6:21 — Where Your Treasure Is

PREPARE
For each child, cut out a paper heart large enough to draw on. I found heart-shaped notepads at a party supply store that worked great. Provide a treasure chest (you can use an old shoebox) and a treasure map (I used a brown paper bag and a black marker). First, I cut a large rectangle out of the brown paper bag. Then I used the marker to draw some of the features of the sanctuary like the pews, the baptismal font, and the piano. Then I drew a big "X" on the map. I even drew a compass rose. And I drew a dotted line that wound around the sanctuary from where the children gather to the big "X". Finally, I crumpled up the map then straightened it to give it a weathered look.

WOW TIME
Prior to the worship service, fill the chest with the paper hearts or notebooks and place the chest in the sanctuary wherever you put the big "X" on the map.

Ahoy, mateys! Guess what? We are going on a treasure hunt! *(Big cheer from the children. Hold up the treasure map.)* I have the treasure map right here. But before we go searching for the treasure, I want you to imagine something. I want you to think of something you did with your family that was so wonderful you remember it to this day. And I don't want you to say it out loud. Just think about that time and let it warm your heart. *(Give them several seconds to do this.)* Next, I want you to think about a time you did something special with a friend. Don't say it out loud. Just think about that time and let the thought of it warm your heart. *(Give them several more seconds.)*

Okay, did everybody think of something? *(Most children will say "Yes." Some might say "No." You may respond by saying, "If you're still having trouble thinking of a special time, that's okay. Most of us can remember more than one special time, so it's hard to choose. You can keep thinking. There's no time-limit on thinking about special times with family and friends.)*

Keep those thoughts in your heads, and those feelings in your hearts. Now, it's time to go on our treasure hunt. *(More cheering. This is what they've been waiting for. Show children the treasure map.)* Let's look at the map. It's the map of a certain room. Can anybody guess which one? *(Some children will say, "This room," or "Right here!")*

That's right. It's a map of this very room. See? Here's the [name places on your own map that correspond to those features in your worship space]. Let's follow the path on the map shown by the dotted lines. That will lead us right to the big "X." Just like all treasure maps, the "X" on our map marks the spot where the treasure is located. Let's go. *(Lead the children around the worship space. Feel free to milk this for all it's worth. Getting to the treasure chest is fun, but half the fun is in the journey.)*

(When you arrive near the spot in the worship space that corresponds to the "X" on your map, say,) According to our map, we should be close. Let's take out our telescopes and look around. Can you see the treasure chest? *(Lead the children in pretending to look through telescopes until someone spots the treasure chest.)*

Avast, ye hearties! We've found the treasure chest! *(By the way, don't feel like you have to do the whole pirate-lingo thing. I just happen to enjoy it.)*

(Open the treasure chest and pull out one of the heart-shaped pieces of paper or heart-shaped notepads). Inside the chest is a wonderful treasure. And look, what shape is that? *(The children will answer, "A heart.")* Where your treasure is, there your heart will be also. Each one of you will get one of these heart-shaped notepads after our prayer. *(The children cheer again.)*

Do you remember when earlier I asked you to think of a time you did something special with your family, and a time you did something special with a friend? *(The children will [hopefully] answer, "Yes.")* I would like you to write about each of those times in your heart-shaped notebook. Or you can draw a picture for each of those times. Then you'll always have a way to remember those special times, and keep them in your heart.

CLOSING
Invite the children to repeat after you each line of the closing prayer. Afterwards, distribute the heart-shaped notebooks.

Dear God,
Help me remember
The things that really matter,
That I may treasure them
In my heart.
Amen.

CHRISTMAS LETTER

THEME
We turn to Jesus for what we really need.

SCRIPTURE
Luke 11: 9-10 — Ask and It Shall Be Given

PREPARE
Acquire a tiny Christmas stocking for each child. The best time to get these is right after Christmas when they are on sale. Inside each little stocking, place a small piece of paper (rolled into a scroll) and a pencil. I used candy cane-shaped pencils (also on sale). Or you can cut out stocking shapes from pieces of construction paper. Many die-cutters even have a Christmas stocking die.

WOW TIME
Merry Christmas! *(Some children may respond with, "Merry Christmas." Others will tell you that Christmas is over, and still others may simply look confused. Many of us are conditioned to think of the Christmas season as running from the Friday after Thanksgiving to 11:59 PM on Christmas Day. In the church year, the Christmas season actually starts on Christmas Day.)*

The Christmas season didn't end on Christmas Day. It's just getting started. On Christmas Day we celebrated the birth of Jesus. Now we get to celebrate that Jesus is alive, and is part of our lives forever. *(Hold up one of the stockings.)* What is this? *(The children will respond, "A stocking.")* And we all know that Santa fills those stockings. *(I purposefully don't ask who fills the stockings. I work with a wide range of ages, and some have more information than others. And the children's moment on the Sunday morning after Christmas isn't where some of that information needs to be shared.)*

Did any of you write letters to Santa asking for what you wanted for Christmas? *(Many children will raise their hands. Some will want to tell you what they got. I recommend you gently move on.)* We ask Santa for what we want. If I want a slinky, I might write a letter to Santa. But I don't really need a slinky. When there is something I feel that I really need, I turn to someone else — Jesus.

Whenever we feel sad and need comfort, we can ask Jesus. Whenever we feel alone, and need a friend, we can ask… *(Indicate for the children to finish, "Jesus."*) When we need help being kind to others, we can ask... (*Allow the children to say, "Jesus."*) When we've made a mistake and need forgiveness, we can ask... (*Allow the children to say, "Jesus."*)

Jesus is the one we turn to for our deepest heartfelt needs. And that's why this is such an exciting time. Even though Christmas Day has come and gone, we can still ask Jesus for what we need. He's with us every day of the year.

(*Show the children the stocking again.*) After we close today, each one of you will get one of these stockings. (*The children cheer.*)

Inside each stocking is a piece of paper and a pencil. Some time today, I want you to think about something you really need. Maybe it's more patience with your little brother. Maybe it's more confidence on the soccer field. Maybe it's finding a way to be a friend for someone who really needs a friend. And you can ask your family to help you with this. You can talk about it over lunch. Then I want you to use the pencil and piece of paper to write a letter to Jesus, asking for that thing. If you'd rather, you can draw a picture of it. And don't worry about where to send the letter. It doesn't have to go to the North Pole. Jesus is with us all the time. We can keep our letters and ask Jesus for what we need by praying to him.

CLOSING
Invite the children to repeat after you each line of the following prayer. Afterwards, distribute the stockings to the children.

Dear Jesus,
Help us remember,
That you are always with us,
And that we can ask you
For what we truly need.
Amen.

BY THE WAY
I know a lot of adults shy away from the whole Santa Claus in church thing. I simply don't share that view. Santa Claus is the concept of someone who goes all over the world to make children happy. He welcomes all children. And he wants us to be good for goodness' sake. Sure, I can tell children "Reason for the Season" and all that other "bumper sticker theology." But I've found that I have the greatest success reaching the children when I meet them where they are, then gently lead them where I want them to go.

Stars

THEME
As big and beautiful as the universe is, each one of us matters to God.

SCRIPTURE
Psalm 8:3-5 — When I Look at the Heavens

PREPARE
You will need an overhead projector. Cut a piece of black card stock to fit exactly over the square glass pane where the light is housed. Before covering the glass pane, use a compass to poke several holes in the card stock. (The point of the compass is just the right size. A safety pin is too small and a pencil is too big.) Then use tape to secure the cardstock over the glass pane of the overhead projector.

Before the worship service, plug in the overhead projector, and place it out of view. You will also need two volunteers for this, one to turn off the lights in the worship space, and one to turn on the overhead projector. The idea here is to make the ceiling of the worship space look light a night sky full of stars. Our sanctuary is very large, so I used two projectors, and had three volunteers. I also spent some time before the service focusing the projectors so that the "star effect" was just right, and not too blurry. We are lucky that even at 11:00 in the morning, we can still control the light in our sanctuary just enough for the stars to project well on our ceiling.

Perhaps your worship space allows so much natural light that this approach simply will not work. In that case, I recommend two things:

1. *Tuck this little children's moment away, and use it for an evening service when the lighting is just right. It's really cool, and a definite "Wow Moment" for the children.*
2. *Adapt this for bright worship space by die-cutting (or hand-cutting) stars from yellow construction paper. Make a bunch! These can then be distributed in the pews, or chairs. At the appropriate time in the children's moment, the congregation can hold up the stars to give the effect of a starry sky. This way takes more work, but the benefit is that it allows the adults to participate. And at our church, the adults will do just about anything for the children.*

You will also need a star sticker for each child.

WoW TiMe

How many of you have ever been outside at night when the stars were really bright? *(Some children will raise their hands. Some will not.)* I'd like you all to lie down and look up. You can spread out some, and give yourselves room. *(Give the children a moment to get situated on the floor.)*

Let's imagine what it would be like to see a sky full of stars right now. Everybody close your eyes — no peeking. We'll count backwards, starting at 10. After we've counted down to one, we can open our eyes. Here we go. 10-9-8-7-6-5-4-3-2-1. *(As the children have their eyes closed and are counting down from 10, have your adult volunteers turn off the lights in the worship space and turn on the overhead projector. When the children open their eyes, let them just look for a few seconds. There will most likely be some Ooh-ing and Ah-ing.)*

Look at all those stars! When I was young I wanted to be an astronaut. I dreamed of floating among the stars. They're so beautiful and bright. But the sky is so wide and so high. And I'm very small compared to all of that. It makes me wonder, "Can someone small like me matter in such a big world?"

But here's the good news — God knows each one of us by name. God knows every hair on our heads. And God loves each one of us very much. The stars may be bright, but so are we, because we are children of God. The stars may be beautiful, but so are we, because we are children of God.

Let's close our eyes once more and count down from 10. Here we go. 10-9-8-7-6-5-4-3-2-1. *(As the children count down from 10 to 1, have the adult volunteers turn off the overhead projector and turn the lights back on in the worship space. If the children are lying down, invite them to sit back up.)*

CloSinG

After our closing prayer today, I'm going to give each of you a star sticker. I want you to wear it all day. And every time you see it I want you to remember that you are, bright, beautiful, and God loves you very much. Our closing will be a call-and-response prayer. I'll say something different each time, and you respond by saying, "I matter to God." Let us pray.

God knows every hair on my head.
Children: **I matter to God.**
God knows every time I've ever laughed.
Children: **I matter to God.**
God knows every tear I've ever shed.

Children: **I matter to God.**
The world may be big, and I may be small, but I know God is always there for me.
Children: **I matter to God.**
Amen.

Calling Nana

THEME
Prayer, communicating with God.

SCRIPTURE:
1 Thessalonians 5:17 — Pray Without Ceasing; Luke 11:1-4 — The Lord's Prayer

PREPARE
You will need to contact a relative (grandparent, parent, aunt, uncle, or even a good friend) a few days in advance. First, ask them if they are willing to participate with you in the children's moment. If they agree to help, request that they stay by their phone during the time of the children's moment, and keep that phone line free. You may even want to have a back-up number, such as a cell phone, just in case. Discuss in advance what topic you will visit about. It could be the weather, a pet, what happened the day before, something simple that can keep the conversation brief. You also need to have a cell phone with you from which to call, and you need to be able to put it on speaker phone. Also, if your worship space uses microphones, use one to help amplify the conversation.

WOW TIME
I have a grandmother who I call "Nana." I love Nana very much. One day, when I was a young boy, I heard someone call her "Mary." Mary?! She's not Mary, she's Nana! A few weeks later I heard someone call her "Mrs. Ivy." And my own mother didn't call her "Nana," but "Mom." I had a hard time with that. She had always just been "Nana" to me, and now I was discovering that she had all these other names, too. But as Nana would say, "It's not about what you call me. Just call me."

Oh, that reminds me — I haven't called Nana in a while. She lives a few hours away. Is it okay if I do that right now? (*You will get a very affirmative response from the children. Dial the number of the family member or friend you are calling. I had Nana's number ready to go. All I had to do was press the "call" button.*)

This was our conversation:

Nana: *Hello?*
Me: *Hi Nana, it's Mark.*

Nana: *Oh hi, Mark.* (as if she didn't know I was going to call)
Me: *I'm with some friends right now, and we called to say hi. Everyone want to say "hi" to Nana?*
The Children: *Hi Nana.*
Nana: *Well hello to you.*
Me: *How have you been?*
Nana: *I've been doing fine. I just got back from church.*
Me: *How was it?*
Nana: *Fine, fine. The sermon was a little long though.* (laughs from the congregation)
Me: *Yeah, that happens sometimes. How are the dogs?*
Nana: *GW and Pearl are doing great. GW keeps chasing after the squirrels, but they're just a little too fast for him.* (giggles from the children)
Me: *Sounds likes you're having a good morning. Well, I better go now. I just wanted to call to say I love you.*
Nana: *I love you too, sweetie.*
Me: *Let's all say "bye" to Nana.*
Children: *Bye Nana.*
Nana: *Good bye. It was nice to talk to you.* (We each hang up.)

You know, there are a lot of names for God. Some call God "Lord." Others call God "Creator" or "Parent." But the most important thing isn't what we call God, it's that we always remember to call. And one of the best ways to call God is to pray. Let's pray together. Repeat after me.

CLOSING
Have the children repeat after you each line of this short prayer.

Dear God,
Thank you for always being there,
Whenever we call.
Even though we might not call
As often as we should,
We love you very much.
And we know you love us.
Talk to you later.
Amen.

BY THE WAY
Everyone loved getting to hear Nana. While most people at my church have never met her, she's become a bit of a celebrity. She is pretty awesome.

"GOD FiRST" TV

THEME
When we put God first in our lives, we think of others, not just ourselves.

SCRIPTURE
Exodus 20:1-3 — No Other Gods Before Me; Ephesians 4:32 — Be kind to One Another

PREPARE
You will need three volunteers who will pantomime a couple of scenes with you. Most of what they do involves standing, and making appropriate facial gestures. Make sure they know what will happen in advance.

WOW TiME

(Have the three volunteers stand next to you.) Today we're going to watch TV. Not just any ordinary TV, but "God First" TV. My friends and I are going to act out a couple of shows. You are in charge of the remote control. Get ready. Press play. *(The volunteers get in a single file line. You start a few paces back. Walk up to the line and look at the three of them standing there. Then go right to the front of the line.)*

(To the children) Press pause on your remotes. Can anybody tell me what was going on in that show? *(Children will answer something along the lines of, "They were standing in a line, and then you cut in front of them.")* I did cut in front of them. Is that something I would do if I was putting God first in my life? *(The children will answer, "No.")*

Okay, here's what I need you to do. First, press the rewind button. *(When the children press the imaginary Rewind button, walk backwards through the scene to your original starting place.)* Now, this time, instead of pressing play, I want you to press the "God First" button. It's right next to the volume. Ready? Go. *(When the children press the imaginary God First button, walk through the previous scene, this time going to the back of the line.)*

When I put God first, I saw the line and went to stand in the back. It was the right thing to do. Let's try another channel. Let's go to channel 23. That's the food channel. *(Have the children press imaginary buttons for 23. While they are doing this, have the volunteers move from a single file line to a group gathered around you.)* Watch this next show carefully. Press play. *(Once the children press play, pantomime the act of receiving a box. Open the box to find a pizza inside. Maybe even smell the pizza. Then slowly pull a slice of pizza out of the box. Make it look like it's really stringy and mozzarella-y. Pretend to blow on the slice to cool it. The other volunteers can see this and look hopeful. Take a few small bites at first. Then dive face first into the box and devour the entire pizza. Then abruptly close the lid on the box and walk away. The other three look dejected.)*

Okay, press pause. What just happened in that show? *(By the way, you can pretend to wipe the crumbs away from your mouth, and ask the question as if your mouth is still full. The children will give the basic gist that you ate a pizza and didn't share any.)* If I put God first, what would I have done differently? *(The children will say, "Share the pizza with your friends.")*

Well let's find out. Please press the rewind button. *(Go backwards through the scene. By far the best part of the bit for the kids is when the pretend pizza goes out of the mouth and back into the box. It's also a little gross, but a little gross every now and then keeps 'em watching.)*

Let's watch the show again, but this time press the "God First" button. Ready? Go. *(The children press the imaginary God First button. You perform the scene again, this time sharing the pizza.)*

When I put God first, I thought about my friends, not just myself. And I shared the pizza. Putting God first means caring about other people, and treating their needs as if they are as important as ours. You can take your remote with you today. Whenever you're in a situation where you're not sure what to do, press the "God First" button and see if that helps.

CLOSING
Invite the children to repeat after you each line of the following short prayer.

Dear God,
Help us remember
To always put you first.
Amen.

communicate

THEME
Prayer is talking with God.

SCRIPTURE
Luke 11:1-4 — The Lord's Prayer

WOW TIME

Let's play a game. I'm going to pretend to communicate with someone, and you have to figure out what I'm doing. Here's the first one. *(Pretend to talk into a phone. Make sure you pretend to listen from time to time. Communication is a two-way street [at least]. The children will guess, "Talking on the phone.")* Right, I was talking on the phone. Here's another one.

(Pretend to write a letter with an imaginary pencil and paper. The children will guess, "Writing a letter," or words to that effect.) I was writing a letter. Well done! How about this? *(Use your thumbs to pretend to send a text. Most children will guess [if you can believe it], "Texting.")* Good job. I was texting. One more. *(Fold hands together and close your eyes. The children will guess, "Praying.")*

That's right, praying is a way we can communicate. Who are we talking with when we pray? *(Most of the children will answer, "God.")* God wants us to communicate with God through prayer. But I have to be honest. The way I just showed you was to help you guess the right answer, but I don't usually pray like that.

There are so many ways to pray. We can pray standing up. Everybody up! *(Have the children stand up with you.)* We can pray with our eyes closed. *(Invite the children to close their eyes.)* We can pray with our eyes open. *(Invite the children to open their eyes.)* We can pray with our hands folded. *(Invite the children to fold their hands.)* We can pray with our hands out, palms facing up. *(Invite the children to stretch out their hands, palms facing up.)* We can pray silently, or out loud. We can sing our prayers, or dance our prayers. The important thing is that we talk with God, and know that God is listening and that God cares.

CLOSING

We can even pray while wiggling. In fact, we are going to close with a wiggle prayer. I'll say the lines of the prayer and you wiggle or pantomime the actions for each line. For example, if I say, "O God who made my fingers," you should wiggle your... *(Allow the children to finish, "Fingers!")* That's it. And if you're in doubt, you can watch me and I'll do the actions with you, okay? Let us pray.

A Wiggle Prayer

O God who made my fingers,
(Wiggle your fingers.)
O God who made my toes,
(Wiggle your toes.)
O God who made my eyebrows,
(Wiggle your eyebrows.)
O God who made my nose,
(Wiggle your nose.)
You made my heart for laughter,
(Put hand to your heart.)
You made my voice for song,
(Make an operatic "singing" pose.)
You made my soul to dance
(Dance or sway in place.)
And praise you all life long.
(Raise both hands high in the air.)
Amen.

You may choose to print this prayer in the bulletin or have it visible on the projection screens.

GOD ROOTS FOR YOU

THEME
We are all God's children, and God loves all of us, no matter what "side" we're on.

SCRIPTURE
Ecclesiastes 9:11 — Time and Chance Happen to All

PREPARE
This is totally optional — wear a baseball or softball uniform. I have a friend who coaches baseball, so this was easy for me. If you'd rather not wear a baseball uniform, at least considering donning a baseball cap, if only for the children's moment.

WOW TIME
When I was younger, I played little league baseball. I was okay, not great, just okay. My friend Sid, on the other hand, was awesome. He was the best pitcher in the whole league, but he played for another team. And when our teams played each other he always struck me out.

The last game of the season was against Sid's team, and just once I wanted to get a hit off him. I took extra batting practice before the game. And I even prayed that I would get a hit. This would be my day!

Why don't you come join me on the field? *(Invite the children to stand and walk in place.)* I want you to feel the soft, green grass beneath your feet. Look up at the big, beautiful blue sky. *(Invite the children to look up and imagine a clear, blue sky.)* The smell of popcorn and hot dogs is in the air. *(Have the children imagine smelling popcorn and hot dogs.)*

I have an idea — why don't you all pretend to be my friend Sid. When I give the go ahead, you pitch the ball, and I'll try to hit it. Let me walk right up to home plate and get my bat ready.

Stand ten to fifteen feet in front of the children in a batter's stance. By the way, I thought of bringing a real baseball bat… then I thought better of it. Me swinging a big bat around a bunch of children is NOT a good idea.

Okay, throw it down the middle. *(Have the children pretend to pitch the imaginary baseball. You must then swing and miss.)*

"Strike one!" shouted the umpire. "That's okay," I thought. "I still have two more chances. Nothing to worry about yet." Then the second pitch came. (*Have the children pretend to throw another pitch, which you swing hard at, only to miss again.*)

"Strike two!" called the umpire. I wish he didn't have to say it so loud. Now I only had one chance left. This was it. Sid reared back and pitched. (*Have the children pretend to pitch one more time. Swing with all your might, only to miss the ball completely.*)

"Strike three!" called the umpire. I struck out. I walked back to the dugout, dragging my bat behind me. Then I sat down on the bench and sulked.

(*Pantomime all of this.*) How could I strike out? I practiced. I prayed. Why did this happen? Was it because I didn't eat my broccoli last night, and God knew it? No, that couldn't be right, because God also knew that I'd helped my brother with his chores.

Was striking out supposed to help me "build character?" But I'd already struck out twenty times that season. How much "character" did I need?

Was it because I didn't pray hard enough? No, that wasn't it. I meant every word of my prayer. I really wanted to hit that ball. But Sid really wanted to strike me out. Hmm, maybe Sid had prayed, too. Did God answer Sid's prayer, but not mine?

But that didn't seem right either. God loved and cared for both of us, and does today. Maybe the real reason I struck out was because Sid just threw the ball a little faster than I swung the bat. God wasn't rooting for one of us to fail and one of us to succeed. What God was rooting for, and what really happened was this — two teams ran out onto the soft, green grass of a field. And with the smell of popcorn and hot dogs in the air, the teams played a baseball game. One side won the game, and one side lost. And in the end both sides shook hands and said, "Good game."

CLOSING

Invite the children to turn to one another and shake hands as they say, "Good game," or "God roots for you." Allow them a several seconds to do this. You may also invite the rest of the congregation to do likewise.

BY THE WAY

Our organist was only too happy to play *Take Me Out to the Ball Game* as the children assembled at the front.

It Was a Dark and Stormy Night

THEME
Sometimes we might get scared, but we know God is always with us.

SCRIPTURE
Psalm 139:11-12 — Darkness Is as Light to You

WOW TIME
Today I'm going to tell a story, and I want you to do all the sound effects. You'll know what sound to make by listening carefully to the story. I'll also point to you to get you started with each sound. Here we go…

It was a dark and stormy night. Timmy was spending the night at his Aunt Lindy's apartment. Aunt Lindy had just tucked Timmy in and turned off the light when Timmy could hear the wind blowing outside. *(Invite the children to make wind sounds by blowing air. You may also choose to invite the entire congregation to participate.)* Raindrops fell against the window. *(Invite the children to make rain sounds by snapping or lightly tapping the fingers of one hand into the palm of the other. By the way, the entire congregation making rain sounds by snapping is way cool.)*

Timmy was starting to feel a little uneasy. Then he heard an owl hooting. *(Invite the children to make hooting owl sounds.)* Timmy pulled the covers all the way up to his chin. Then he heard the old grandfather clock right outside in the hall. *(Invite the children to make tic-tock sounds.)*

Everything seemed so strange in this strange place, even Aunt Lindy. Timmy could hear her in the next room playing some strange song on her trombone. *(Invite the children to make the sound of a trombone sliding down and up on "Waa.")*

Worst of all, there was a lump on the floor. Timmy couldn't figure out what it was. But that lump, combined with all the strange sounds was too much. He sat straight up in bed and yelled out, "Aunt Lindy, Aunt Lindy!" Immediately the trombone music stopped, and Aunt Lindy rushed into Timmy's room. She turned on the light as she entered. "Timmy, what's wrong?" she asked.

Timmy told her all about the strange noises and the lump on the floor. "The lump on the floor?" she asked. Then they both looked over to the floor, and with the light on, they could see what it really was — a pile of Aunt Lindy's dirty socks. Timmy and Aunt Lindy giggled a little.

She turned back to Timmy and said, "It's okay to be scared. We all get scared sometimes. One of the things that makes me feel better is praying. It's one way I remember that, even when I get scared, God is with me. Here's a little prayer I know. You can repeat each line after me."

Say the prayer, and have the children repeat each line after you.
Thank you God, for wrapping me
In the blanket of your care.
Thank you God, for caressing me
With the night-light of your grace.
Thank you God, for soothing me
With the lullaby of your love.
Amen.

After they prayed, Aunt Lindy asked, "Can I get you anything — a glass of water, maybe?" Timmy smiled, said he was fine, and thought he might be ready to go to sleep. Aunt Lindy gave him a big hug, and turned out the light as she left.

Timmy said the prayer his aunt taught him one more time. As he closed his eyes, he could still hear the same sounds he had before. The wind was still blowing. *(Invite the children to make wind sounds.)* The raindrops kept tapping at the window. *(Invite the children to make rain sounds.)* The owl kept hooting. *(Invite the children to make owl sounds.)* And the grandfather clock kept tic-tocking. *(Invite the children to make tic-tock sounds.)* But none of these sounds bothered him anymore. He knew what they were, and they even seemed soothing now. And the strangest sound of them all, Aunt Lindy's trombone playing, was also the most soothing. Timmy wasn't sure he was hearing things correctly, but it sounded like she was trying to play him a lullaby. *(Invite the children to make trombone sounds. You could lead them in a few bars of Brahms'* Lullaby *or* Twinkle, Twinkle, Little Star.*)*

And within minutes, Little… Timmy… fell… asleep. *(Invite the children to make snoring sounds.)*

CLOSING
Repeat the prayer from the story and have the children repeat each line after you.

GOD'S RAINBOW

THEME
All of us are different. All of us are special. All of us are part of God's colorful family.

SCRIPTURE
1 Corinthians 12:14-20 — Many Members, Yet One Body

PREPARE
You will need a small plastic bracelet for each child. Each bracelet should be of a single color, and there should be multiple colors represented by the different bracelets. Party supply stores usually carry inexpensive packs of bracelets such as these. You may prefer to make bracelets from paper strips in an assortment of colors.

WOW TIME
(Start by giving each child a bracelet, and inviting them to put their bracelets on.) Today we're going to see what God's rainbow looks like. Everybody make sure you have your bracelets on. And if you would rather have a different color, maybe you can trade with someone else after worship.

First, anyone with a yellow bracelet, hold it up for us to see. *(The children wearing yellow bracelets hold up their hands so the others can see.)* Yellow is a beautiful color. But it's only one color. We can't make a rainbow with yellow alone. Okay, you can put your hands down.

Anyone with a purple bracelet, hold it up for us to see. *(The children wearing purple bracelets hold up their hands so the others can see.)* Purple is a beautiful color. But it's only one color. We can't make a rainbow with purple alone.

(Continue this with every other color represented by a bracelet. Then say,) Each color is beautiful. But each color, by itself, cannot make a rainbow. What can we do to make a rainbow? *(Most children will have an idea, such as, "We have to put all the colors together.")*

Everyone who has a bracelet of any color, hold it up so all can see. *(All the children raise their hands to show their bracelets of different colors.)* This is what God's rainbow looks like — all the colors coming together to make something more beautiful than one color could ever make by itself.

CLOSING

Today we are going to close with two simple call-and-response prayers. For the first prayer, I will say something different each time, and you always respond with "Thank you God, for Different." Let us pray.

Thank You God, for Different

Some are short, some are tall.
Thank you God, for Different.
Some play banjo, some play ball.
Thank you God, for Different.
Some are quiet, some make noise.
Thank you God, for Different.

Some are girls and some are boys.
Thank you God, for Different.
Some like pizza, some like yam.
Thank you God, for Different.
Some like honey, some like jam.
Thank you God, for Different.

Now I'll say something different each time, and you always respond with, "Thank you God, for Same." Let us pray.

Thank You God, for Same

We all share the stars above.
Thank you God, for Same.
We all share your endless love.
Thank you God, for Same.
We all see the sun and rain.
Thank you God, for Same.
We all feel life's joy and pain.

Thank you God, for Same.
We are family through your Son.
Thank you God, for Same.
We are many, we are one.
Thank you God, for Same.
Amen.

DIFFERENT/SAME

I've actually had the opportunity to use this children's moment twice – once with children at my home church in Fort Worth, Texas, and once while I was working with children in Kenya. On the outside, the two groups of children could not have appeared any more different. But the children from both hemispheres liked the bracelets, and really got into the spirit of the message. In fact the children in Kenya, when they all raised their hands together to make the rainbow, began clapping for each other. They got it.

GRUDGES

THEME
Holding a grudge does more harm than good.

SCRIPTURE
Ephesians 4:26 — Do Not Let the Sun Go Down on Your Anger

WOW TIME
Let's imagine we're having a nice day at school. *(Invite the children to stand and walk in place with you.)* We're walking down the hall, minding our own business, when Buddy bumps into us. *(Have children stop.)*

Buddy doesn't say "Sorry" or "Excuse me." He just walks right on by. That's it! We're going to hold a grudge against Buddy. That means we're going to be mad at Buddy, and keep being mad. Now grudges are kind of heavy, but it's only one grudge. Everyone hold on to your grudge, and we'll keep going. *(Invite the children to continue walking with you, but a little heavier, as if carrying something bulky.)*

Next, we're going to the cafeteria for lunch. We go through the line only to find that it's Brussels Sprouts Day. Yuck! We can't stand Brussels sprouts. Now we're going to hold a grudge against whoever made up the school menu. That makes two grudges now. Let's keep going. *(Invite the children to walk with you, even slower and heavier. The weight of the two grudges is pretty noticeable.)*

It's been a pretty rough day. But when we get home, we call our best friend to set up a play-date. *(Invite the children to join you in pretending to call a friend.)* But when your friend answers the phone, you find out that she already has someone over to play. You hang up the phone and say, "I thought we were best friends." That's it! Now you're going to hold a grudge against your "former" best friend. *(Invite the children to join you in hanging up the phone and picking up another grudge to carry around.)*

So now we have three grudges we're carrying around – one against Buddy, one against the person who put Brussels sprouts on the cafeteria menu, and one against our "former" best friend. *(Invite the children to walk in place very heavily while carrying all three grudges.)*

Wow! These grudges are really heavy. Who's having the hardest time with all these grudges, them or us? *(The children will answer, "Us.")*

Exactly. When we carry all these grudges around, it makes us feel heavier and heavier until we can barely walk. It doesn't do anybody any good. One of the best things we can do for ourselves, and for others, is to let go of our grudges. Let's start by letting go of all these grudges we're carrying right now. One, two, three, drop them! *(Have the children pretend to drop all the grudges, and stand taller and lighter).*

Ah. That feels better already. Letting go of grudges always feels better. When we let go of our grudges, it's a way of showing forgiveness for others. And that makes God feel better, too.

CLOSING
Lead the children through the process of the following grudge prayer.

I want you to think of someone who has made you really mad. Don't say it out loud, just think about that person. Maybe you're still holding a grudge against that person. I want you to put your hand over your heart, right where you think that grudge might be.

Next, I want you to gently rub right over your heart until you can feel that grudge in your hand. *(Give the children a few seconds to do this.)* Now I want you to pull that grudge away from your heart and hold it tightly in your hand. As you hold it, I want you to repeat after me:

God forgives,
And so can I.
I forgive.
Amen.

Gently open your hand out flat. And with one soft breath, blow that grudge up into the air, away from you forever. Wave goodbye to your grudge. It's gone. Amen.

CHOOSE

THEME
Following God's way is always the right choice.

SCRIPTURE
Psalm 119:30 — I chose the way of faithfulness; Joshua 24:14-15 — Choose this day whom you will serve

PREPARE
Decorate a medium-sized cardboard box with elaborate designs, paper, and bows. Inside the medium-sized box place two smaller boxes, one marked "Box A" and one marked "Box B." These small boxes remain empty.

Get an assortment of star stickers, or other small prizes, enough for each child to get one. (It doesn't really matter too much. This children's moment is more about the process than the prize.) Put an equal number of stickers in each of two small brown paper bags, marked "Bag 1" and "Bag 2" respectively. Place these two small paper bags in a larger brown paper bag. It will help if the larger brown paper bag is very wrinkled and weathered looking.

WOW TIME
Today is all about making choices. *(Show the decorated box and the wrinkled paper bag.)* We have a box and a bag. Let's choose which one to open. *(Most will choose the elaborately decorated box, and that's key. If the majority choose the bag [which is highly unlikely] you can override and go for the box. The good thing about this happening is that you, rather than the children, are the one responsible for a making a poor initial choice.)*

Great. Let's open up the box. *(Open the box. Take your time and really milk this.)* Hmm. Isn't that interesting. Inside this box are two smaller boxes. *(Take out the two smaller boxes so the children can see.)* It looks like we have a Box A, and a Box B. Which one should we open? You choose. *(You may get an equal number of votes for each box. Pick the one that you feel got the most support and open it.)* There's nothing in this box. It's empty. What should we do? *(Most of the children will say something like, "Look in the other box.)* That's a great idea. Let's look in the other box. *(Look inside and reveal that it, too, is empty.)*

Well, that is very odd. Both boxes were empty. What should we do? *(A few of the children might suggest, "Let's look in the bag.")* I agree. Let's look in the bag. *(Open the bag and take out the two smaller bags.)* It looks like we have Bag 1 and Bag 2. You choose. Which one should we open?" *(Open whichever bag got the most votes. Reach in and pull out a handful of star stickers or whatever prizes you placed in the small bags. There may very well be cheering from the children.)*

I think you made a great choice. There were stickers in this bag. Way to go! You know, I'm a little curious. I wonder what would've happened if we'd opened the other bag first. What do you think? *(Some will want to see what happens if we open the other bag. Others will be convinced that it is empty since the stickers were in the other bag. Reach in and pull out a handful of star stickers. Some of the children may be surprised by this.)*

There are stickers in this bag, too. Since there were stickers in each of the small bags, all we had to do was make the right choice at the start. If we had chosen the wrinkled brown bag in the beginning, then no matter what we chose after that, we would've found stickers.

And when we choose to follow God's way from the start, it can make the choices after that much easier. The right choice isn't always the prettiest choice, but it's always right.

After our closing, each one of you will get a star sticker. When you wear it I want you to remember the importance of good choices.

Closing
Have the children repeat after you each line of the following short prayer.

Loving God, help us be strong,
In choosing right instead of wrong.
Help us live a life that's true,
And choose what you want us to do.
Amen.

Easter Egg Hunt

THEME
Easter is a day when we celebrate the resurrection of Jesus.

SCRIPTURE
Matthew 28:1-10 — The Resurrection of Jesus

PREPARE
Okay, this one's a bit involved. But hey, it's Easter. Get small plastic Easter eggs, enough for each child. Place a small plastic butterfly inside each egg.

Provide three larger plastic eggs. Draw a picture of a white Easter lily on a sheet of white paper (or find one online). Cut the picture into three strips, and place each strip inside of one of the large eggs. Prior to the service, hand each large egg to an adult helper in the congregation. Each helper will hold up an Easter egg at the appropriate time in the children's moment. Make sure the volunteers know the order in which each is to hold up the egg. (Having the three large eggs be of different colors will make this much easier.) And choose volunteers in different spots. That will make it more fun than having all three volunteers sitting together.

Also prior to the worship service, put all the small Easter eggs with the butterflies inside in a large basket. Place the basket behind some Easter lilies in the worship space, out of view from the children.

WOW TIME
Happy Easter! This is a day we celebrate Jesus rising from the dead. Jesus lives forever, and Jesus' love lives forever. That's good news. Easter is also the day we get to have an Easter egg hunt. *(There will be lots of cheering for this.)* There are Easter eggs scattered all over the worship space. It's up to us to find them. I want you to stay right where you are, and keep your eyes open. Let me know when you see *(make this next part obvious for your adult helpers)* the blue egg. *(At that cue, the helper with the blue egg [or whatever egg you indicate] should hold it up so the children can see it. Within seconds, many excited children will be pointing with shouts of, "There it is!" Run over to get the blue egg from the helper and bring it back to where the children are.)*

Great! You found the Easter egg. Let's see what's inside. *(Open the egg and pull out the strip of paper inside.)* Hm. That's odd. It's just a piece of paper. There's part of a design, but I can't tell what it is. Oh well. I'll hold on to it while we look for more Easter eggs. See if you can spot a green egg. *(The helper with the green egg should take that as the cue to hold it up so the children can see it. Immediately you'll hear, "There it is!" Hurry off to get the green egg and bring it back to where the children are.)*

What excellent Easter egg hunters you are. Let's see what's inside this one. *(Open the egg and pull out the strip of paper.)* It's another piece of paper with part of a design on it. Not very exciting. Well, let's keep looking. Let me know when you spot the orange egg. *(That's the cue for the helper with the orange egg to hold it up for the children to see. The children will point and yell, "There it is!" Go get the orange egg and bring it back to where the children are.)*

Excellent. You found another egg. Let's see what's inside. *(Open it up and pull out the strip of paper.)* More paper. I wonder if there are any more eggs. *(Look out among the congregation. When you see no more eggs, appear dejected.)*

Bummer. That's only three Easter eggs, and there are so many of you. *(Look down at the three slips of paper you have.)* Hey! Look at this. These aren't just three pieces of paper. They're pieces of a puzzle. *(Take a few seconds to put the pieces together. A couple of pieces of tape wouldn't hurt. Show the picture to the children.)* Look. It's a picture. Does anyone know what this is? *(Some children will call the lily by name. Others will look around, and maybe point to the lilies in the worship space.)* I think you're right. It's a picture of an Easter lily. *(Pause for a few seconds to build suspense.)* I wonder… if maybe… just maybe… this might be a clue… *(Walk over to the lily, reach behind, and bring out the basket with all the small eggs in it. This will most likely draw a huge cheer from the children. Bring the basket back to where the children are.)*

Now that's more like it! I knew there had to be more Easter eggs around here somewhere. *(Open an egg and show what's inside.)* There's a butterfly in each egg *(and a Scripture if you choose to put that in as well)*. Butterflies remind us that Jesus rose on Easter day. And it looks like we have just enough eggs for each one of you to have one. *(More cheers from the children.)*

CLOSING
Before I hand out the Easter eggs, let's close with a special call-and-response prayer for Easter. I'll say something different each time and you always respond by saying, "Hallelujah!" Let us pray.

Christ is alive.
Children: **Hallelujah!**
Love is alive.
Children: **Hallelujah!**

Hope is alive.
Children: **Hallelujah!**
We are alive.
Children: **Hallelujah!**

"Fear Not" Freeze Tag

THEME
When we are frozen by fear, we must remember that God is with us, calling us to action.

SCRIPTURE
Four "Fear Not" Scriptures : Genesis 46:3 —Jacob Bringing His Family Down to Egypt to Meet Joseph; Isaiah 43:1,2 — When You Pass Through the Waters; Luke 2:10 — The Angel Announces to the Shepherds the Birth of Jesus; Luke 5:10 — Jesus Calls the First Disciples

WOW TIME
Today we are going to play a game called "Fear Not" Freeze Tag. The words "fear not" appear in the Bible many times, because there were many times when people were scared. And when they were scared, they would often freeze. But God or Jesus or even an angel would tell them, "Fear not." This was a way of unfreezing the people who were scared so they could do what God needed them to do or go where God needed them to go. In the game "Fear Not" Freeze Tag, every time you hear me say "freeze" you must freeze in whatever position you're in. And when you hear me say "fear not" you can unfreeze and continue moving.

Let's all stand up and pretend we're walking through the desert. *(Lead the children to stand and walk in place. Maybe even pretend to wipe the sweat away from your face, and fan yourself.)* We're on our way to Egypt to apologize to our brother. We were really mean and picked on him a lot. Now our brother is very powerful, and we're afraid he's going to get us back. We get so scared that we **freeze**. *(Have the children freeze, holding whatever walking position they are in.)* But God tells us "**Fear not**, for I will go with you to Egypt." *(Lead the children to unfreeze and keep walking.)* So we finally make it to Egypt, and our brother forgives us, and welcomes us into his home.

Now let's imagine we're shepherds out in a field keeping watch over our flock at night. *(Lead the children to stand guard, and look around as if watching for danger. Maybe even invite a few children to make sheep sounds.)* Then an angel of the Lord appears, and we get so scared that we **freeze**. *(Lead the* *children to freeze in place.)* But the angel says, "**Fear not**, for behold, I bring you good tidings of great joy."*(Have the children unfreeze.)* The angel tells us that Jesus has just been born, and we should go to Bethlehem to see him. So we run as fast as our shepherd feet can go. *(Lead the children to run in place.)*

Now let's imagine we are out fishing. *(Lead the children to pretend they are fishing. You can use imaginary fishing poles, that's fine.)* But we're not catching anything. Then Jesus walks up and tells us where we can go to catch lots of fish. We row our boat out to where he tells us. *(Have the children pretend to row a boat.)* We start fishing again, and before we know it, we're catching all kinds of fish. We catch so many that we're worried it may sink our boat. And how did Jesus know where to find all the fish? All the thoughts swirl around in our head and we get scared and **freeze** *(Have the children freeze.)* But Jesus says, "**Fear not**. Follow me and I will help you catch people." *(Have the children unfreeze, and row some more.)* So we row to shore, leave our boats behind, and follow Jesus. *(Have the children walk in place.)* **Freeze.** *(Have the children freeze.)*

Sometimes we can get so scared that we can't move. It's almost like our feet don't remember how to work. But God has big plans for us. There is so much to do, and there are so many places to go. And all along the way God is saying, "**Fear not**, I will be with you." *(Have the children unfreeze.)*

CLoSiNG
Say the following prayer on behalf of all who are gathered.

Dear God,
There is so much you need us to do in this world.
But sometimes we can get really scared,
So scared that we freeze.
Thank you for reminding us to fear not,
For you are with us every step of the way.
Amen.

Connect the Dots

THEME
As members of God's family, we are all connected.

SCRIPTURE
Romans 12:5 — We Are Members One of Another

PREPARE
This one requires a good bit of preparation, but the end result is very exciting. This is a children's moment they'll remember. In terms of materials, you'll need 7 to 14 index cards, a green marker, and a blue marker.

The rest of the preparation involves knowing your congregation. It is your task to figure out what individuals have in common with one another. You also must ensure that these individual members will be at worship. Adapt to fit your setting.

WOW TIME
Prior to worship, I used the index cards and markers to make a green set of cards numbered 1-2 and a blue set numbered 1-5. I used the church directory to help figure out which member had specific things in common with other members. I also needed to make sure the members I chose would be at worship. I also tried to include members who typically sit far apart from one another in the worship space. This would make the overall effect more powerful. I knew that our children's choir would be singing, so that helped me identify people who would definitely be there.

Right before the service, I handed out the numbered cards to the people I had identified. I then coached each person to listen closely for when to stand and hold up their number. Exactly who those people were will become apparent in the following.

Today we are going to play one of my favorite games — "Connect the Dots." But look at how big our sanctuary is. *(The children looked around.)* This is a big space, and dots are so small. Instead of playing "Connect the Dots" with actual dots, we're going to use people.

Let's start with the green version of "Connect the Dots." Who's holding the green number 1? *(Aaron, our organist stood up, holding the green 1 card, and said, "I am." I ran up to the organ and said,)* Aaron is holding the green number 1. He is our organist. Every week he uses his talents to glorify God and inspire us. Who is holding the green number 2? *(Sara, the* children's choir accompanist, held up the green number 2 card, and said, "I am." All the children enjoyed this, especially those in the choir. Sara is someone they all know and love. I ran over to Sara at the piano and said), Sara is holding the green number 2. She also uses her talents to glorify God and inspire us. See how Sara and Aaron are connected? (Most of the children said, "Yes.")

That was an easy one. Now let's try "Connect the Dots" with the blue numbers. Who has the blue number 1? (Aerin, a member of the children's choir held up the blue number 1 and said, "I do." I went over to Aerin and said,) Aerin is the blue number 1. She is a member of the children's choir. Who has the blue number 2? (Emma, also in the children's choir held up the blue number 2 and said, "I do." I went over to Emma and said), Emma has the blue number 2. She is also a member of the children's choir. That's how she is connected to Aerin. Emma has a birthday on February 8th. Who has the blue number 3? (Mrs. Maurer, from way in the back of the sanctuary, held up her blue number 3 and said, "I do." I ran to the back of the sanctuary, to the delight of the children, and said,) Mrs. Maurer has the blue number 3. She also has a birthday on February 8th. And Mrs. Maurer taught piano for sixty years. Who has the blue number 4? (Katie, a teenager sitting about ten rows up from Mrs. Maurer, stood up with her blue number 4, and said, "I do." I ran over to Katie and said,) Katie has the blue number 4. She practices piano every day. Mrs. Maurer would be very proud of her. Who has the blue number 5? (Sara, the Children's Choir accompanist, held up the blue number 5 and said, "I do." The children were beside themselves. I ran back down to the front to Sara, and said,) And Sara has the blue number 5. She, like Katie plays the piano. Did you see how everyone with the blue numbers was somehow connected? (The children said, "Yes.") And isn't it interesting that there was more than one path that led back to Sara? (The children thought that was very cool.)

So you see? We are all connected. Even though it may not always look like it from the outside, we are one family under God.

CLꞶSiNG
Invite the children to repeat after you each line of the following short prayer.

Dear God,
Help us remember
That we are all one family.
We are all connected to each other,
Because we are all connected to you.
Amen.

ESTHER

THEME
We can have courage to do the right thing, because God is with us.

SCRIPTURE
Esther, particularly Esther 4:8-17 — Esther Agrees to Help Her People

BACKGROUND
During the Jewish festival, Purim, the story of Esther is read. It is tradition to use noisemakers called "graggers" to make noise each time Haman's name is read, so that no one will hear his name. This concept has been adapted here so that each person in the story is represented by a sound.

WOW TIME
Today we are going to tell the story of a very brave woman from the Bible named Esther. I will tell the story itself, and I want you to help by making sound effects to go along with the story.

There are five main people in this story and each one of them will have their own accompanying sound. Every time you hear the name Xerxes, make a trumpet sound. Let's practice… Xerxes! (Have the children make trumpet sounds. It can be a 4-note fanfare or a general cacophony.)

Excellent. When you hear the name Vashti, make a lip pop sound. Let's practice that one… Vashti. (Have the children make lip pop sounds.)

When you hear the name Mordecai, clap your hands. Mordecai. (Have the children clap.)

When you hear the name Haman, stomp very loudly. Haman's the bad guy in our story. Haman! (Have the children stomp. They'll really get into that one.)

And finally, the heroine of our story. Whenever you hear the name Esther, shout 'Hooray.' Let's try it… Esther. (Have the children shout "Hooray!")

Great. Keep your listening ears open. Here we go. (Read the following story. When you come to a name in bold print, say it, and then pause for a second so the children can make the corresponding sound. You may want to help them by doing the sounds with them, at least at first.)

ESTHER – A MUSICAL SOUND EFFECTS STORY

Xerxes, the king of Persia, held a big feast. Xerxes sent for his wife, Vashti, so that everyone could see her. But Vashti refused to come, and that made Xerxes very mad. He declared that Vashti would not be queen anymore, and that he would choose a new wife from many beautiful women.

One of these women was Esther; she was an orphan who had been adopted by Mordecai, a Jewish man who worked in the palace. King Xerxes fell in love with Esther and married her, not knowing she was Jewish.

Haman, the king's second in command, hated Mordecai, and wanted to get rid of all the Jewish people. Mordecai discovered Haman's plot and asked Esther to tell King Xerxes about it.

Esther was very nervous. She would be in big trouble if she went to King Xerxes without being invited. But she found the courage to invite King Xerxes to a banquet the next day.

That same night, Xerxes remembered that Mordecai had once saved his life. He wanted to reward Mordecai and asked Haman for advice. Haman thought King Xerxes wished to reward him, so he advised that the reward should be to ride in a procession wearing royal clothes. King Xerxes liked the idea. "All right!" he said, "Prepare all this for Mordecai."

Haman was very upset. He wanted to get rid of Mordecai, not honor him. That evening at the banquet, Esther revealed to King Xerxes that she was Jewish, and that Haman was planning to get rid of her people.

King Xerxes punished Haman and rewarded Mordecai with a royal procession. King Xerxes then gave Haman's job to Mordecai. It was a great day for the Jewish people, thanks to the bravery of Esther!

CLOSING
Invite the children to repeat after you each line of the following prayer.

Dear God,
Help us remember
That we can be brave
And do amazing things
Because you are with us
Every step of the way.
Amen.